Presented to the
Tulsa City-County Library
by

tulsa
LIBRARY TRUST

OKLAHOMA BEER

A Handcrafted History

BRIAN WELZBACHER
Foreword by Wes Alexander

Published by American Palate
A Division of The History Press
Charleston, SC
www.historypress.com

Copyright © 2022 by Brian Welzbacher
All rights reserved

First published 2022

ISBN 9781540250926

Library of Congress Control Number: 2021949215

Notice: The information in this book is true and complete to the best of our knowledge. It is offered without guarantee on the part of the author or The History Press. The author and The History Press disclaim all liability in connection with the use of this book.

All rights reserved. No part of this book may be reproduced or transmitted in any form whatsoever without prior written permission from the publisher except in the case of brief quotations embodied in critical articles and reviews.

For Cora and Rainn.

"Do every act of your life as if it were your last."
—*Marcus Aurelius*

CONTENTS

Foreword, by Wes Alexander	7
Preface	11
Acknowledgements	13
Prologue	15
Nomadic Roots, 1889–1907	19
Prohibition Was Choc-Full of Beer, 1907–1933	26
Oklahoma Brewing Progresses, 1933–1976	31
All's Quiet on the Plains, 1976–1992	48
Belly Up to the Brewpubs, 1992–2003	51
A Craft of Their Own, 2003–2015	92
The Oklahoma Beer Boom of 2016	152
Afterword	161
Appendix: Oklahoma Brewery Directory	167
Bibliography	177
About the Author	191

FOREWORD

As you will read in this book, Oklahoma craft beer has a story to tell that parallels our state's history. Hardships, pioneering spirit and stories that seem made for the movies are the ingredients for the craft story in Oklahoma, which is admittedly short but nonetheless interesting. In the end, Oklahoma stands tall and proud with more than forty small independent brewers pumping out world-class beer.

It hasn't always been easy. My experience with the craft beer industry began in 2007 at Marshall Brewing Company. At that time, we had a few brewpubs in the Oklahoma City area that were producing 3.2 percent ABW beers for sale on-premise, as well as our dear friends at Choc Beer Company in Krebs, Oklahoma, operating the only full-strength production brewery in the state at the time. While the craft beer industry was in full swing nationwide, only a small audience of enthusiasts and homebrewers were familiar with what Marshall Brewing had planned for the marketplace. In my role as director of marketing at sales at Marshall, it was immediately apparent that many retailers and consumers assumed that we were brewing in buckets. Little did they know that Oklahoma was on the cusp of a boom in professionally planned production breweries spanning the state.

Early adopters who brought in kegs of Marshall such as Empire Bar, McNellie's Pub and Soundpony Bar were crucial in the development of the understanding of craft beer. Many of these retailers came by the brewery to learn about our processes, see the equipment and watch Eric Marshall work feverishly by himself brewing and packaging our beer. That knowledge was then conveyed to patrons of those establishments. I cannot thank enough bartenders like Joel Bein at the Empire Bar, who took extra care sampling patrons and sharing our story with a passion that equaled our own. This, then, is the story of Oklahoma. The little state that could—a flyover state filled with entrepreneurs with the unmistakable can-do spirit that best characterizes Oklahoma. When I reflect on the hardships of my own family—be it the Dust Bowl or oil and gas booms and subsequent busts—I see a roadmap to perseverance necessary to make our state work as well as the craft beer industry.

I would be lying if I didn't admit that in those early days at Marshall Brewing, we were naïve. One of the biggest issues we faced had to do with the perception of beer itself in Oklahoma. Since the late 1950s, Oklahoma had been a so-called 3.2 percent beer state. What this meant, though, wasn't always clear to consumers. Was beer from other states stronger and therefore better? Was Marshall brewing and selling 3.2 percent beer? While neither of these assumptions was true, they had been culturally ingrained in generations. Undoing the 3.2 percent culture took patient education.

One of the biggest hurdles facing craft brewing pioneers from 2000 to 2016 was sampling and selling beer on site at breweries. Perhaps the largest contributing factor to the growth of craft beer in America has been the opportunity for consumers to visit breweries—the opportunity to sample and purchase craft beer while visiting with the folks who worked at the brewery about styles, processes and ingredients that built loyal grass-roots audiences. In Oklahoma, brewers producing so-called strong beer (in excess of 3.2 percent ABW) were prohibited by law from sampling or selling beer on site. One of my favorite/least favorite anecdotes of this era happened at nearly every brewery in Oklahoma. Out-of-state craft beer enthusiasts would travel through Oklahoma, stop at a brewery and enter with enthusiasm only to find that they could not, in fact, sample or purchase beer at the brewery. One gentleman was so taken aback that he barked at me, "Well, should I expect that I can't purchase bread from a bakery in Oklahoma as well?"

Speaking of naïveté, surely the sampling issue in Oklahoma could be resolved legislatively, right? It took more than three years of handshaking and begging to get our state legislature to take a serious look at sampling for production brewers in Oklahoma. Finally, in 2013, the craft beer industry found a champion of fairness in business in State Representative Glen Mulready (R.). Unbelievably, the wine industry in Oklahoma was permitted sampling and direct sales of products at on-site operations. Opposition to the HB 1341, permitting brewers to sample on-premise, was strong. In

Foreword

Sales and Marketing Director Wes Alexander gives guests a brewery tour in December 2013. *Photo by the author.*

committee, sample size (which was planned at sixteen ounces per person per day, or the equivalent of one pint of beer) was trimmed to twelve ounces. In the end, Glen's leadership, as well as a mobile and active grass-roots group of activists willing to call so frequently in support of HB 1341 that they caused an outage of the phone lines at the capitol, got the job done. That simple act, allowing brewers the opportunity to sample their beer on site, seemingly was the keystone of modernization in Oklahoma. Today, visitors to our state would barely notice any difference in how beer is conveyed in comparison with other states.

We've come a long way in Oklahoma with respect to craft beer. Gone are the days of consumers asking what craft beer would be most like Bud Light. In and around 2010, Marshall would host events at bars and restaurants featuring cask-conditioned ale served from a firkin (a small keg that is manually tapped). In the short span of a year, consumers went from asking what a firkin was to asking what was in the firkin. Visit a beer festival in Oklahoma today and you will find thousands of craft beer enthusiasts well versed in styles, ingredients and techniques. So, where does the craft beer

Foreword

in Oklahoma go from here? My challenge to brewers and consumers alike is to continue to tell the story of craft beer to those unfamiliar with craft beer. I remember the excitement and world of possibilities that opened for me when I was introduced to a Boston lager in the late '90s. Most craft beer enthusiasts have a similar story. We should all endeavor to continue sharing our passion for craft beer with others. As successful as craft beer is, it represents just over 12 percent of all beer sold in the United States. That number should be 20 percent and growing.

Craft beer has been responsible for revitalizing urban areas and breathing new life in aging neighborhoods across Oklahoma. Craft beer provides valuable jobs in manufacturing in Oklahoma. The economic impact of craft beer in Oklahoma was estimated at $465 million in 2016. Oklahoma, since the discovery of oil outside Tulsa in Glenn's Pool, has had an economy closely tied to the volatility of the oil and gas market. Meanwhile, craft beer offers sustainable growth and jobs year after year.

Finally, it is worth noting that Marshall Brewing, and every other craft brewery in our state, would not have enjoyed the success we have without the cooperation and support of everyone involved. In the early days, Joe Prichard and Michael Lalli at Choc Beer Company mentored us. Although consumers aren't usually privy to these stories of cooperation, they are well known in the brewing community. The logistical challenges and growing pains associated with operating a brewery sometimes lead to outages of ingredients such as malt or crowns for packaging beer. When these challenges are presented, Oklahoma brewers step in to help fill the gap for fellow brewers. That spirit of support and generosity is owed to Joe and Michael. In the end, it's what my grandfather called being neighborly. That's what we do here in Oklahoma!

—Wes Alexander,
Sales & Marketing Director,
Marshall Brewing Company

PREFACE

Oklahoma has been referred to as a "flyover" state for countless years regarding the alcohol industry. Since I moved to Tulsa in 2008 from Illinois, the state was barren when it came to quality beer, let alone high-ABV beer choices. Once I learned about the state's unique alcohol laws—involving liquor stores being closed on Sundays, 3.2 beer and there being hardly any breweries around—my world dramatically changed. So, why did this guy who grew up with St. Louis in his backyard decide to write about Oklahoma's beer history, you ask? You could say I was in the right place at the right time, bearing witness to the slow yet budding rise of the craft brewing industry. My first Oklahoma beer was also considered the state's first beer, Choc, from Krebs Brewing Company. One hazy ale that slaked the thirst on a hot summer's day while attending a Tulsa Drillers minor-league baseball game and I was hooked into learning more. From there, I took a trip with friends down to Krebs for a brewery tour, with expectations I was accustomed to in St. Louis. Upon inquiry about a tour, the staff just looked at us oddly, but one of the brewers understood our interest and showed us around the small brewhouse.

I immersed myself early on as the craft beer scene ramped up steadily around the United States. Soon, Marshall Brewing Company in Tulsa came online, and there was a spark of energy in the city. As the years progressed, I found other likeminded imbibers who appreciated the handcrafted movement and wanted more from their adult beverages than yellow fizzy water. I created a company called Beer Is OK in 2012 to band together

Preface

fellow lovers of the craft and to support these local breweries that were up and coming. My enthusiasm led to the creation of a blog and eventually a podcast that covered all things Oklahoma beer. I then collected an oral history from many of the breweries and from those in the early homebrewing stages that transitioned to the big leagues. Little by little, I worked my way into the brewing scene of Oklahoma and made friendships with those in the industry, learning the hardships they had to go through with the archaic laws that kept others from taking risks. I recall early on people asking why it is this way and complaining of inconvenience, but I could never get a straight answer as to why.

In this book, we will discuss Oklahoma's brewing history as a whole state since a good bit of it is intertwined between the metropolitan hubs of Oklahoma City and Tulsa. At the time of this writing, the craft brewing market is surging at an exponential rate, with major constitutional changes on August 24, 2016, breaking the chains of belated prohibition. We will touch on many new breweries that have endeavored to educate and change the mindset of closed-minded thinking from the past. While most stories will be told, this book in no way will be complete; instead, it will serve as a deep look into the origins of Oklahoma's subtle yet integral part in the history of America's rich brewing culture.

ACKNOWLEDGEMENTS

While there is only one name on the cover, this book would not have been possible without myriad people. I'd first like to thank Arcadia Publishing and The History Press for reaching out and realizing that Oklahoma has a rich story to tell in the world of brewing. Its professionalism and patience while I slowly built out this book while tackling my own job and family life is greatly appreciated. Never in my wildest dreams would I have thought that I could tackle such a massive task as writing a book. I am forever grateful to all the brewers who were so inviting to a guy who was transported from the rich beer culture of St. Louis to the barren plains of Oklahoma. I enjoyed blogging, podcasting and writing for the *Southwest Brewing News*, all while igniting lasting friendships in the beer industry as an enthusiast and advocate.

I figured that blogging and podcasting was a great way to capture the culture and history of Oklahoma's beer scene like those who preceded me. I thank the beer writers and reporters who recorded the early days of brewpubs and craft breweries. The invaluable archive of the *Southwest Brewing News* (*SWBN*) bimonthly papers, loaned to me from Jeff Swearengin, gave this book a backbone and insight into the early struggles that brewpubs faced. More recently, I want to thank Nick Trougakos of the *Thirsty Beagle* blog and Tom Gilbert of the *What the Ale* blog from the *Tulsa World*. Your tireless efforts made the beer industry more transparent and gave breweries a voice to the masses that would otherwise have gone unheeded. I thank the historical societies and archivists like Steve DeFrange for his dedication to the Krebs History Museum and preserving the story of Choc beer.

Acknowledgements

As a graphic designer, I would be remiss if I did not thank all those who provided visually stimulating images that help tell the story of Oklahoma brewing. To the breweriana and antique collectors, thank you for preserving pieces of history that would otherwise be buried in the past due to Oklahoma's short-lived brewing industry. To the families of past brewers like Sean Ahrens, your archives helped tremendously in telling the exciting yet heartbreaking tale of Ahrens Brewing Company. To the North American Guild of Beer Writers and its members, I thank you for your encouragement and wisdom that helped me along while I stumbled in the dark. The same thanks goes to Zephyr Adventures and the Beer Now conference, where I met other beer writers, bloggers and enthusiasts who enriched my passion to write this book.

I would like to thank my closest friends and family, like my parents, who constantly asked how the book was going. It was those unwarranted prods that kept me going. To my friends and fellow enthusiasts who helped me edit and provide suggestions along the way, your guidance was needed more than you'll ever know. And finally, to my wife, Amy, who has been my rock ever since I told her about this crazy idea so many years ago. You provided me the time, space, patience, love and understanding needed to pursue such a wild endeavor. Your love knows no bounds, and I owe you a long, all-inclusive beach vacation. Also, thanks go to my kids, Cora and Rainn, who reminded me that I need to take a break to play every once in a while.

PROLOGUE

Brand new state—gonna treat you great!
Gonna bring you barley, carrots and pertaters,
Pasture for the cattle, spinach and termaters,
Flowers on the prairie where the June bugs zoom,
Plen'y of air and plen'y of room,
Plen'y of room to swing a rope!
Plen'y of heart and plen'y of hope.
—*lyrics from the song "Oklahoma"*

The Compromise of 1850 kicked off a rousing story about an unsettled land that paints a picture of the real Wild West. In 1850, Texas ceded land back to the United States. Some four years later, the Kansas and Nebraska borders were defined by the 36th and 37th parallels thanks to the Missouri Compromise of 1820, which had forbidden slavery above the 36½ parallel; thus, a strip of land was left over to be known as "Public Land Strip." This 170 miles of uninhabited prairie that the Santa Fe Trail went through would eventually become the panhandle of Oklahoma. The lands mainly served as a throughway for cattlemen driving their herds up north to Kansas. Cherokees laid claim to the neutral lands for several years until the secretary of the interior established the area as public domain. By 1886, settlement had become prevalent across the plains of "No Man's Land." This land without any governmental law spawned a refuge for the lawless and destitute over time. Countless stories tell of folks taking vigilante actions, as one resident explained it: "There was no court expenses, no long drawn-out trials; no delays; no appeals; no dockets; no paroles; no pardons." In 1888, the Rock Island Railroad founded a town called Tyrone in which to load up cattle stock. A heavy run of cowboys and cattlemen needed an outlet for their rowdiness out of Liberal, Kansas, where the railyard lay. The infamous Carry Nation had dried up Kansas fairly well with her Anti-Saloon League and created the demand for a city to form near the border to slake the thirst of the cattle herders.

As swift as a scissortail, a bunch of canvas tents went up, and White City was born three miles south of the border to provide an outlet for boisterous ranchers who needed a drink. The name was soon changed to Beer City on account of the stacked barrels of beer sitting outside the saloons with names like the White Elephant and Yellow Snake. One Kansas newsman reported it thus: "There were eight to 10 saloons, a number of gambling houses and several bawdy houses to represent the business industries of Strip city." Women from Dodge City and Wichita would come down from Liberal to make a hefty wage entertaining the men who drove through. Aptly dubbed the "Sodom and Gomorrah of the Plains," Beer City was a party 24/7 and held "stage dances, horse races, boxing and wrestling matches" as well as Wild West shows to keep guests entertained between drinks. The most famous story was about Pussy Cat Nell, the leading madam who ran the Yellow Snake tavern; she was fed up with a self-proclaimed marshal by the name of Lew "Brushy" Bush who would go to all the businesses and demand protection money for his services. Refusing to pay, Nell was roughed up by the offender, and most of the townsfolk were soon fed up with his actions. When he came around to collect the next time, she shot him down, and several others joined in to ensure that not one person was accused of his murder.

For more respectable people, it was hard to make a living, as crops were poor and many of the crude drifters had left after a severe drought in 1888. Thousands of residents fled to the east after the famous land run of 1889 consisted of settlers claiming Indian territory to establish what would eventually become Oklahoma Territory after the Oklahoma Organic Act of 1890. In lieu of waiting on a signal, many restless settlers were called "Sooners," hence the Sooner State nickname. The eastern region of Oklahoma served as reservation lands for Native Americans due to the passage of the Indian Removal Act. The Choctaw tribe signed the Treaty of Dancing Rabbit Creek, yielding most of their 11 million acres in central Mississippi to roughly 7 million acres in the southeastern corner of Oklahoma. Like the many immigrants who ventured overseas to find a new

PROLOGUE

Beer City, No Man's Land. This prairie haven of rest and relaxation for the cowboys of the Oklahoma and Texas Panhandles was called "The Sodom and Gommorah of the Plains." Lew Bush, the town Marshal, who was shotgunned to death by Madam Pussy Cat Nell, sits next to the standing fiddler. Photo taken in front of The Elephant Saloon on June 25, 1888.

Beer City attracted thirsty cowboys on the prairie. Some were drawn to the town's saloons, the Elephant Saloon and the Yellow Snake Saloon, June 25, 1888. *Courtesy of Western History Collections, University of Oklahoma Libraries.*

way of life, the tribe brought their beliefs and culture to the eastern portion of Oklahoma Territory. While its origins are somewhat mixed, a homebrewed concoction called "Choc beer" was birthed out of the mining towns and became a popular bootlegged drink among miners and railroad workers. Originally brewed by the Choctaw tribe, recipes were altered to each person's liking based on what they had available to them. An 1894 report to Congress listed one recipe as a "compound of barley, hops, tobacco, fish berries, and a small amount of alcohol." The federal government had put a ban on all alcohol in the Indian territories dating back to 1803. However, the legal jargon was misconstrued with the term "spirituous liquor," which provided a loophole to continue production of Choc beer. It was not until 1895 that the U.S. Congress banned any manufacturing or the sale of "vinous, malt or fermented drinks of any kind" in Indian territory. A long heritage of dry counties in Indian territory ties into the temperance movements and how Oklahoma became the only dry state to enter the Union.

Despite the regulations, members of law enforcement continued to raid establishments for making alcoholic products (often under pseudonyms like "Rochester Tonic," "hop ale" or "Malt Nutrines"). There is also the story of how "Pussyfoot" Johnson, a deputy U.S. marshal, helped coin the phrase "bootlegger" after stopping a traveler moving through Indian territory and finding illegal whiskey in the man's boot. As travelers began to populate the state, and leading up to statehood, there were a few brewers established in Oklahoma City. Naturally, the large oil boom in Tulsa at Red Fork flooded the area in 1901 and brought in all kinds of outside investors who made Tulsa their home. These Indian territories, as they were labeled in 1834, continuously shrank over time, and in 1890, the Oklahoma Enabling Act was signed by Theodore Roosevelt to combine Oklahoma and Indian territory. This led to Oklahoma becoming the forty-sixth state in the Union in November 1907.

NOMADIC ROOTS, 1889-1907

Oklahomans will vote dry as long as they can stagger to the polls.
—*Will Rogers, humorist, cowboy and performer*

Imagine a fertile, untouched prairie in the middle of the country rife with resources and potential to create a new future for yourself. With the crack of a pistol, everything changes. After the Unassigned Lands of Oklahoma were finally ceded by the Creek Nation, settlers found their way onto the land by any means necessary, and like a fine, handcrafted beer, they built up this land from scratch. Thus the "Land Run" of 1889 set the stage for major development, and folks seeking a better way of life came to Oklahoma Territory. Tent cities were erected immediately in places like Oklahoma City, Norman, Stillwater and others on that fateful day of April 22. Prior to statehood, alcohol was prevalent in the territory. The original name of Elk City, Oklahoma, was Crowe, but it was changed to Busch in the hopes of luring Adolphus Busch to build a brewery in the newly developed town. "However, when the brewery did not materialize, the name was officially changed in 1901," as stated on VisitElkCity.com.

The state took shape from then on as the rail systems were quickly constructed. It seemed as though most intoxicants were imported from Milwaukee, St. Louis and surrounding states at the beginning. About a decade after the land run, there were a few breweries that took shape due to outside interests to serve a growing territory. Planning had begun in 1900 as B.B. Moss of Chicago announced plans to erect the largest brewery

Beer, Cider, Ginger Ale, Mineral Water, Etc.

"Oklahoma's Best," Celebrated Moss Beers. both bottled and draught.
MOSS BREWING COMPANY.

"Ok'a" Draught and Bottled Beer.
OKLAHOMA ICE AND BREWING CO.

Iron Still Cider, Ginger Ale, Mineral Water, Sarsaparilla and Soda Water of all kinds.
NEW STATE BOTTLING WORKS.

Ginger Ale, Iron and Sarsaparilla Phosphates, Ironbrew, and all Up-to-date Carbonated Beverages.
OKLAHOMA CITY BOTTLING WORKS.

Advertisement from the *Daily Oklahoman* for local brewery products, October 18, 1904. *From newspapers.com.*

in the Southwest, costing about $200,000. All machinery—the boiler, refrigeration, engines, coolers, vats and more—was purchased in Chicago; the brewery would have a capacity of twenty-five thousand barrels and employ about thirty people. Plans to sow acres of land for barley were considered if they could produce about thirty thousand bushels. If so, Moss would invest in a malt house and be in the business of manufacturing malt as well. By March 1901, Moss announced that beer could be ready by May 1, as brewing equipment was being installed "from the sixth floor to the basement to receive malt and other materials that will make the first beer brewed in Oklahoma Territory," as stated in an op ed in the *Daily Oklahoman* on March 10, 1901. About a year later, in February 1902, Moss Brewing was incorporated by B.B. Moss, John Wild and William Scherer, with a capital stock of $75,000. The men went on to produce cider, ginger ale and mineral water, per an advertisement in 1904. A small op ed in 1907 claimed them as the pioneer brewery in Oklahoma City that produced "46 Star" and "Moss Draught Beer."

On April 12, 1902, Mr. A. Ruemmeli of St. Louis declared in the *Daily Oklahoman*, "We have just organized a charter for the Oklahoma Ice & Brewing Company with a capital stock of $250,000 for the purpose of manufacturing ice, doing a general cold storage business, manufacturing malt liquors, and also manufacturing electric light and power. The capacity of this plant will be 75,000 barrels per year. We expect to do a very large shipping business and to make Oklahoma City a distributing point for the southwestern territory." He mentioned prominent men interested in this enterprise, including Mr. Adolphus Busch, Wm. J. Lemp and Mr. Pabst, yet

A Handcrafted History

Oklahoma Ice & Brewing Company at Third and Santa Fe. *Courtesy Max Pritschow, Mrs. Collection, Oklahoma Historical Society Research Division.*

he did not go into detail about their involvement. The new development was located between Second and Third Streets, Broadway and the Santa Fe tracks in Oklahoma City. The major portion of this block being erected was the Oklahoma Ice & Brewing Company plant, built by George Pankau of St. Louis, who later supervised the construction of large buildings for the 1904 World's Fair City.

After a year and a half of development, on October 20, 1903, manager J.B. Murphy of the Oklahoma Ice & Brewing Company submitted an application for a liquor license in the *Daily Oklahoman* newspaper. Thus the "Largest Building in the Southwest" was open to Oklahoma and the Indian territories on November 8, 1903, where it manufactured "Beer that Will Make Oklahoma City Famous." The new industry was taking shape, employing local residents and taking pride in its work, like one would see today with the slogan Oklahoma Beer for Oklahomans. Details of exactly what was being brewed weren't clear. OK'A beer appeared to be the first brew, destined to give "Oklahoma City fame as the Milwaukee of the southwest," as stated on January 31, 1904, in the *Daily Oklahoman*. Adolphus Busch was elected its first president in early 1904, leading some to think that this could set up a possible transition to the brewing plant becoming a distributor of Anheuser-Busch. Such wasn't the case, although business continued to be successful as it expanded in 1905 and produced a bock beer. To remain competitive, it reduced the price to ten cents per bottle to "put the price within the reach of all," restating the fact that it was a local manufacturer and undercutting the competition, which shipped its beer in from out of state. Here's an early sense of pulling back the curtain, a transparency we see so prevalent in the craft beer world.

For all its success, the brewery was short-lived, exchanging hands with another St. Louis businessman, H.Y. Thompson. The nature of the sale is unclear, but the vice-president, A. Ruemmeli, who was acting as a personal representative of Mr. Adolphus Busch, came to inspect the properties and handle the sale. Mr. Thompson applied for a new liquor license on February 11, 1905, as receiver of Oklahoma Ice & Brewing Company and renamed it the New State Brewing Association. Apparently, the Anheuser-Busch Brewing Association had taken ownership and then sold it to Thompson some months later. E.F. Clauss was elected general manager and a personal representative of Adolphus Busch, so there still remained some interest in the property. Around this time, Busch was looking to expand his brewing operations in the untouched lands of the Southwest, as the North and Midwest were already overrun with breweries. Along with many improvements and an enlargement of the cold storage capacity, Anheuser-Busch supplied its brewing chemist to inspect the plant for possible improvements. In December 1905, the large cold storage house suffered an incendiary fire, causing more than $50,000 worth of building and property damages. The city had been going through a bout of low water pressure, so when fire crews arrived, it was like David versus Goliath, as they were armed only with buckets of water found at

A Handcrafted History

Oklahoma Ice & Brewing Company opening announcement from November 8, 1903. *From newspapers.com.*

the brewery. Flames spread and ravaged on into the afternoon until it was decided "as a last resort" to unload two large vats of beer that would eventually extinguish the flames.

Operations appeared to be successful, as an optimistic ad in the October 28, 1906 *Daily Oklahoman* invited readers to use New State Beer "not alone as a drink, but as a food product as well." Although we can't know what the beer would taste like today, the same ad described the beer as "rarely delightful flavor, the rich amber color, and the glorious, sparkling, snapping, creamy foam, please the eye and the palate." How's that for descriptive advertising? Around this time, the talk of statehood was ramping up, and fear of the state entering the Union under prohibition was taking off. New State was under the gun to testify that its product was more than an intoxicating beverage, as it was viewed by the Anti-Saloon League and Woman's Christian Temperance Union. Several large ads in late 1906 extolled its beer as the "foremost temperance drink," containing less than 4 percent alcohol and less

Oklahoma Beer

Above: Oklahoma Ice & Brewing Company bock beer ad, March 7, 1905. *From newspapers.com.*

Left: New State Brewing Association advertisement from July 29, 1906. *From newspapers.com.*

Opposite: New State Brewing postcard. *From taverntrove.com.*

alcohol than pure apple cider, which was more readily available and easier to produce. An ad from the October 14, 1906 *Daily Oklahoman* goes even deeper, claiming that its beer promotes healthier digestion by "increasing the secretions of the digestive organs and aids in the assimilation of food, and by doing so is conducive to good health." Beer certainly contained few contaminants, and being brewed from naturally occurring ingredients led some to think of it as a food product.

A Handcrafted History

However, the temperance leagues had lumped all products into their campaign to have prohibition written into the Oklahoma constitution. Their fight was tenacious, and not long after Oklahomans accepted prohibition in the new state, the ironically named New State Beer Association declared that it would officially quit the production of beer. It took about two days to dump twenty-seven thousand gallons of beer down the gutters (valued at about $75,000 at the time). One reporter for the *Daily Oklahoman* noted, "As it spouted from the hoses into the gutter, one man was unable to find a cup or a bucket. He lay contentedly on the sidewalk and drank from the stream as it flowed past him." The plant was eventually turned into a cold storage facility and ice manufacturer. The Moss Brewery met a similar fate and was seized by the state in 1908. They were forced to dump 1,000 barrels of beer that cost nearly $8,000. President H.Y. Thompson remained optimistic, even though the state that he tried to build up economically had turned on him. "The most profitable part of our business has been destroyed by prohibition, but I have great faith in Oklahoma City and will do everything possible to advance the growth of the town," Thompson told the *Daily Oklahoman* on September 21, 1907.

PROHIBITION WAS CHOC-FULL OF BEER, 1907-1933

*A pint's a pound the world around, but if it is Choctaw beer
it more nearly approximates a ton.*
—Hartshorne Sun

On May 25, 1908, two boys were arrested for breaking into a United States post office looking for food, admitting they drank "Chock" beer. "We had a keg of Chock," claimed one of the boys in the *Daily Oklahoman*, confirming that it contained yeast, malt and sugar. According to them, it was easy to make and everyone around Wilburton (a Choctaw mining district) did so. The story of "Choc" beer is about as hazy as the unfiltered wheat beer that shared the same name of the one brewed by Krebs Brewing Company. There is the all-too-famous story of an Italian immigrant named Pietro Piegari who was brought up in the coal mining town of Krebs. At the tender age of eleven, he worked the mines until a tragic accident ended his mining career. While bouncing around through odd jobs, he took up homebrewing. Legend has it that the Choctaw Indians had a recipe utilizing the local wheat grown in Oklahoma. Thus the name "Choc" was used, representing the beer and the brewing process. The beer was brewed in an old crock until it slaked his thirst properly, and Pietro served it alongside meals to local miners out of his home. The coal industry of southeast Oklahoma brought in many European immigrants who suffered harsh times in their native homes. They adapted and kept traditions alive like cooking, winemaking and sharing family traditions. Pietro, who

A Handcrafted History

A statue of Pete Prichard stands in front of Pete's Place in Krebs, Oklahoma. *Photo by Tom Gilbert/ Tulsa World.*

later changed his name to Pete Prichard, cooked hearty Italian meals for the miners with a mix of frontier food and old-world Italian classics, starting up the business that still stands today known as Pete's Place.

As entrepreneurial and inspiring as this venture was, it was highly illegal, and Pete went to jail several times for selling beer during Prohibition. He and countless others in Oklahoma were subjected to the prohibitory laws instituted into the state in 1907. The Choc epidemic slowly rose up as more people of working-class stature and minorities were continually busted for brewing and selling the intoxicant. Early reports from a *Daily Oklahoman* article in 1912 stated that Choc beer was a drink "readily made from such conglomerations as malt, cornmeal, and raisins," or that other extreme ingredients like axle grease were added to give it the necessary "kick." Debates stirred on whether it was a harmless table drink or a dangerous intoxicant among the district and county courts. Newspapers were littered with stories across the state over decades of raids on Choc beer joints and dumping of Choc beer. One account stated that several hundred barrels were emptied into Oklahoma City sewers in 1915. It grew so bad that in May 1918, a ban was placed on the sale of malt and restriction on the sale of sugar by the state food administration. It was estimated that 1.7 million pounds of sugar were being used to make Choc beer. Don Pulchny, grandson of "The Polander," recalled in the documentary film *Blue Smoke*, "My grandfather was injured in the mines and needed to find a way to make a living. He would make Choc and catch frogs in Lake Eufaula and sell the Choc and frog legs to make his living." Much like the Prichards, Mike Pulchny would host senators, judges and lawyers over the years, to the point that his living room was transformed into a bar, according to his grandson. "His way around selling it was putting out a donation jar and people knew that if they wanted 3 quarts of cold Choc they had to put in a dollar."

Pittsburgh County held some of the richest deposits of coal, spanning some one hundred miles to the Arkansas border. "A majority of the Italians that came here and worked in the mines were from central Italy where economic times were pretty depressed and they came here looking for a better life," said Steve DeFrange, curator of Krebs History Museum. Many other people of European descent came as well, bringing their customs and ways of life, which included making beer and wine to have with their meals. Making these libations was an escape from the hardships of mining, as the probability of coming home was low due to the dangerous nature of the job. "Many times the wives would have to start making and selling Choc to help support their family if their husbands were killed in the mines," added Steve. Ingredients were plentiful and could easily be obtained from local stores. Choc was cheap to brew, and most people used old crocks and cast-iron pots that they'd also use for other daily chores. The most common process was filling a pillowcase with grains and hops, being sure that the bag didn't sink to the bottom. Once the mixture cooled, people would transport that to a ferment jar and transfer to bottles once it was ready to drink. According to Sam Lovera of Lovera's Grocery in Krebs, "If it was made right, when you open it, blue smoke would come out of the bottle." Around the 1950s, there were still "Choc Joints" that you could just walk into and be offered a glass of Choc, even to kids in their early teens.

The temperance movement to eliminate drunkenness and keep intoxicants out of the hands of Native Americans resulted in Choc beer as an unintended consequence. One news article out of Muskogee dived into the nature of Choc beer and how it "Beats Real Beer" (meaning Budweiser), from some folks who were asked about it. Most recipes clocked in at 6 percent alcohol, and it became harder for law enforcement to crack down on producers because those drinking it were not heavily intoxicated. The numbers of public drunkenness cases dwindled because it was harder to catch people drinking the beer. It harkens back to true homebrewing in the kitchen, where small batches were easy to make for personal consumption or sold for a high profit. There is an excellent book that documents the struggles of how law enforcement tackled bootlegging in Oklahoma called *Grappling with Demon Rum*, by James E. Klein. It recounts the history of Oklahomans in a cultural battle where middle-class Prohibitionists demonized public drinking to instill pure ethics and morals by shaming the working class. This was successfully implemented by institutions like the Anti-Saloon League and Woman's Temperance Christian Union, which had the ear of Congress and lobbyists during statehood and national Prohibition. The Progressive movement was also taking shape, as women were serving as advocates for family health and wanted to end the widespread sale of liquor that was taking hold of the budding nation. Much of this came about on a national level, as many southern states had abolished liquor altogether and went dry well before Oklahoma became a state. Historically, Americans' choice of drink was distilled liquor; there was not much of a culture that involved beer until German immigrants brought over their practice of lager brewing in the early 1800s. German culture embraced beer as an easy drink to have with a meal and family gatherings. However, most Americans were found in rough whiskey joints and looked down on by those of higher class during the temperance movement, which promised to bring an end to poverty, crime and domestic abuse.

Eventually, the Volstead Act, also known as the National Prohibition Act of 1919, brought about one of the darkest eras in U.S. history according to some. The Eighteenth Amendment and national Prohibition halted brewing operations and saw copious amounts of beer and liquor dumped. Naturally, Oklahoma was unphased by this measure, going through its own turmoil to curb bootlegging and corruption with its own people. Unfortunately, no one thought to examine the results of Prohibition and the unintended consequences that followed. Americans found ways around the law to get their liquor and beer by homebrewing and bootlegging. Eventually, the opposition won, and the Twenty-First Amendment was passed in April 1933. However, each state had to also pass its own legislation to legalize the sale of 3.2 beer, and Oklahoma dragged its feet. First, the House drafted a bill, but the Senate wanted to wait on the bill from the District of Columbia to assist in writing up a different bill that would include taxation and places where 3.2 beer can be sold. In late March, a new prohibition proposal appeared in a bill by William Coe, Oklahoma County, for a referendum to decide if the state constitution should be modified on what defines an intoxicating liquor. With this new bill, people could initiate a petition to change the prohibition section to allow the sale of intoxicants but forbade use on-premises where sold. Meanwhile, nine other states were ready to sell beer on April 7. The beer bill was voted on by the House, barely winning in a 60-54 vote. The measure, which levied a tax on 3.2 percent beer as non-intoxicating, then went to the Senate. If it had been enacted, it would have gone into effect ninety days after adjournment. Opponents could then take it to the people for a referendum.

The Senate made a full redraft of the beer bill, demanding a straight vote. A special committee was formed of seven senators to rewrite the bill after drys in the Senate failed to send it to a prohibition committee and let it die. Overall, the bill asked to "prohibit the sale of anything intoxicating over 0.5% except in restaurants, cafes, hotels and regularly operated clubs that have been open more than 2 months." Before the large debate over the new referendum, more than $7.5 million was generated in beer sales, along with new jobs created nationally since Prohibition was lifted. At this time, the fate of the bill was uncertain. Wets received twenty-one votes but needed twenty-three. What proceeded was a four-hour-long debate, often claimed as the state's most spectacular in legislative history.

Members of the public filled the stands, and many were turned away, as there wasn't a seat left, with many cheering for beer. It came down to the Anti-Saloon League arguing the constitutionality of the referendum and what determines an intoxicating beverage. At this point, it was raised to 3.2 percent, nullifying that defense. Another key element was the use of tax revenue for public school funding. The House passed a bill calling for a special election to be set for July 11, and the wets were tasked with funding it, as ordered by Governor Murray. In anticipation of the referendum passing, Progress Brewing Company and Tulsa Brewing Company paid $606 in taxes, and wholesalers and retailers filed licenses and ordered train carloads of beer. Without much surprise, the beer referendum won by more than 100,000 votes. The governor ordered the National Guard to patrol the rail yard under martial law to prevent early unloading of beer before the celebration. This was the beginning of Oklahoma and its famous "3.2" beer, which was allowed to be made and sold in the state.

OKLAHOMA BREWING PROGRESSES, 1933-1976

SOUTHWESTERN BREWING CORPORATION/PETER FOX BREWING (1933–1946)

Coming out of Prohibition, several breweries came online and produced local beer for hardworking Oklahomans again. Being granted the first federal and state license in Oklahoma, the Southwestern Brewing Corporation was first in line with its Old King beer. The name is a reference to the state abbreviation, with quality fit for a king. Another coincidence in the royalty reference was the facility, which was the former home of the "king of beers" Anheuser-Busch, which sold it to New State Brewing, right before Prohibition. Custom-built equipment was crafted with certain specifications in mind for the brewers working there. A new venture like this employed hundreds of citizens who desperately needed jobs after the Great Depression.

The brewery was owned by a nonnative to Oklahoma, Nicholas A. Schlangen, who was also an owner of Imperial Brewing Company in Grand Rapids, Michigan. He had an extensive background in the brewing industry, as his father owned Schlangen Manufacturing Company of Chicago and manufactured brewery equipment in the United States. An engineer by trade, Nicholas also contributed several inventions to the industry. Nathan S. Blumberg served as counsel and a corporate lawyer who oversaw many of Schlangen's breweries.

The leading factor in these breweries, beyond making an enjoyable product for the masses, was the massive tax revenue for the state. The first

Left: Old King Beer & Vienna Beer ad from April 23, 1939. *From newspapers.com.*

Above: Old King Pilsener Beer crown cap of Southwestern Brewing Corporation. *From taverntrove.com.*

year predicted almost $1 million between the state and federal taxes paid out. Another important fact presented to the public in a *Daily Oklahoman* exposé was that beer was classed and taxed as a food item by the Pure Food and Drug Act of 1906. This remained true, as 3.2 beer by weight (or 4 percent by volume) was taxed as a food product in Oklahoma. Old King beer was labeled as a pilsner; numerous brewers were flown in to consult and assist in the "tests" of the beer to dial in the perfect recipe.

The president, Moses Iralson, saw great potential for economic proliferation during Oklahoma's time as a territory. He built the first mercantile building in Lawton and established the first department store there in 1901. Southwestern enjoyed a good run, selling more than 48 million bottles of Old King beer by June 1937. Competition was not a huge factor, and it created a local product that was a key component in its sales and marketing. Over the years, it added other products, like Golden Vienna to commemorate the golden anniversary of the state of Oklahoma in 1939. An ad for Old King and Gold Seal Premium beer in 1942 touted the benefits of purified air by use of ultraviolet rays. Other beers brewed included Old King Pilsner Winter Beer, Black Dallas Beer, Old King New Blend Extra Dry and Bock Beer.

A Handcrafted History

Above: Old King's 2 millionth case. *From the Clarence and Willie Ford Collection, Oklahoma Historical Society Research Division.*

Left: Old King Beer ad from September 23, 1934. *From newspapers.com.*

Fox DeLuxe Beer label (*left*) and Silver Fox Beer label (*right*) of Peter Fox Brewing Company of Oklahoma City. *From taverntrove.com.*

Although the first brewery in Oklahoma had a great run, it was acquired by Peter Fox Brewing of Chicago in June 1946. Rolling out with its Silver Fox DeLuxe Beer, PFB advertised its historical link to Oklahoma as going back to 1908. It started with peaches and soon engaged in the butter, egg and poultry business on a large scale. The Fox group joined in the oil boom of 1943 and played a pivotal role in discovering the West Edmond oil field. Brewing since 1933, Fox breweries were franchised around the country, producing more than 1 million barrels per year. The 150,000-barrel plant was renamed the Peter Fox Brewing Company of Oklahoma, and additions likely doubled the capacity for the chain. In a full-size ad in the *Daily Oklahoman* on August 25, 1946, the brewery highlighted new and improved ingredients like Bohemian hops and "exclusive pure culture yeast." Operations continued with several hiccups, including the Second World War and a large warehouse fire causing more than $75,000 in damages. Old King is remembered to this day by Bricktown Brewery, which created an Old King Kolsch, served in classic fishbowl chalices.

Progress Brewing Company/Lone Star Brewing (1934–1976)

Like many immigrants who came into the United States, John Francis Kroutil emigrated with his parents from Czechoslovakia in 1881. He was a pioneer of business leaders in Yukon, serving as president of the Yukon National Bank, president of the Yukon Electric Company in 1907 and

Progress Brewery postcard. *Courtesy of Western History Collections, University of Oklahoma Libraries.*

president of the Yukon Mill and Grain Company, leading it into the beer business. John realized that when 3.2 beer would be legalized, he wanted to create one of the finest plants for brewing beer in the nation. Business partner and vice-president G.F. Streich began operations in the spring of 1934 on Fourth and Douglas, a key location to deliver products economically and efficiently to its retailers. To achieve his vision of a modern plant, they employed the services of George Lehle of Chicago, a nationally recognized brewery architect, to design it, and Macdonald Engineering Company of Chicago constructed the plant, sparing no expense. Ground was broken on September 20, 1933, continuously expanding to construct the deep-water wells, power plant and modern brewing equipment. It was completed in December 1934, and beer had been brewed and aged in preparation for the grand opening. Truly built from the ground up, no other brewery could compare to its scale and passion for a quality local beer that was owned, operated and financed by Oklahomans.

Along with a catchy slogan, "Where there is Progress—you will find Progress Beer," the company truly led the budding brewing industry in its 165,000-square-foot, six-story building, which produced 100,000 barrels per year at its peak. Placed on a spacious tract of ten acres, the massive brewery became touted as the most modern in the state, with the use of

150,000 gallons of water pumped by seven electric motors into storage tanks daily. The plant housed three cellars of twenty cold storage tanks, totaling 10,000 barrels housed on the upper floors of the plant. Progress used a gravity system to transfer the beer from cypress wood fermenting tanks to the storage cellar, where it sat for about sixty days at a temperature of thirty-three degrees. The final step sent the beer to a finishing cellar for more aging and then to the bottling and keg filling stations. Of course, no brewery was complete without a skillful master running the operations to consistently produce the beer.

Otto Deter started in the brewing industry as an apprentice at the age of fifteen and amassed more than forty years of brewing experience as a journeyman in Europe. Deter stated that the art of brewing is in the science and that a true quality beer was measured by high-quality ingredients and the skill of the master brewer. As a student of Pasteur, he set a very high standard in the art of fermentation and did not think highly of the other "beers" being distributed around the country. By this stage in his career, he had already brewed in New Jersey and Oregon and owned a brewery in San Francisco. A new endeavor with Progress allowed him to be in full control of a massive brewery as its master brewer. Assisting Deter was Paul Pechstein, who came from a family of well-known brewers.

Progress Beer Fully Aged Lager bottle. *Photo by the author.*

On April 10, 1935, numerous state officials and legislators were invited to an open house to celebrate the opening of the brewery and the start of distribution. Landscape architects beautified the lands with juniper shrubs and young trees to give an air of freshness compared to that of the mellow brew being crafted inside. Among those visiting, C.A. Nowak, editor of *Modern Brewery* in St. Louis, considered the brewery an "exceptionally modern and complete plant." Eventually, the plant was opened to the public to experience the process of beer brewing. Progress beer was truly a beer for Oklahomans, as distribution was wholly focused on fulfilling Oklahoma demand before distributing out of state. It went so far as turning down

A Handcrafted History

contracts from five hundred to one thousand cases per day just so local drinkers had the first crack at the brew. Oklahoma City was the central distribution point, followed by Tulsa, supplying a large warehouse as well as twenty-two wholesalers to take care of the other wet counties in Oklahoma. After a full year of producing its mellow lager in 1936, Progress paid more than $1 million in federal and state taxes, which provided funding to local schools; had employment for nearly 14,500 people in various capacities; and purchased as many supplies as it could to keep it a local Oklahoma product. Progress employed a new brewmaster, John J. Giesen, who held more than forty years of experience in brewing, dating back to his time in Indianapolis. In 1905, he founded and served as the brewmaster for Capitol City Brewing until he sold his interests and the company in 1915. He had won medals in Brussels, Paris and London for prize beer.

Oklahoma's Own Select Progress Beer bottle. *Photo by the author.*

In 1938, an ad appeared in the *Daily Oklahoman* for "An Ideal Spring Tonic Drink," advertising a new bock beer. Described as a heavier-bodied brew, the bock beer was created as a winter beverage that was supposedly richer in flavor. A new beer emerged called Progress Select Beer that touted the finest ingredients possible: "There's a barrel of quality in every bottle." An ad in 1939 gave the public a transparent description of how a high-quality product at an affordable price of only ten cents per bottle could be made—by controlling distribution within the state, brewing massive volumes at a time and using high-grade machinery.

Around 1940, an ad placed in the *Daily Oklahoman* was addressed to Oklahoma beer retailers in an attempt to clean up the so-called eyesores that were using "their permits as a mask for illegal practices." The Oklahoma Brewers and Beer Distributors Committee assisted local law enforcement in weeding out these objectionable dealers and keeping its business pure. Places like these were called "honky-tonks," and another ad brought awareness of illegal activities such as gambling, bootlegging and selling to minors. Beer received a bad reputation under these establishments, and the committee had helped weed out more than one hundred honky-tonks by 1942. Leading into the Second World War, Progress Brewing put out several ads touching on low product supplies and promoting the sale of stamps and war bonds. In an effort to meet the financial needs of the state in 1945, a beer tax raised the price of a barrel to ten dollars and increased bottle prices to an average of about sixteen cents.

Everything was progressing well for the brewery until June 12, 1954, when John Kroutil suffered a life-ending heart attack at his farm near Piedmont. He left behind a legacy through building up companies from scratch during a revolutionary time in Oklahoma. He was a very active leader in the community through the Knights of Columbus and Yukon City Council. His partner, Streich, had already passed away, and ownership was under question. Talks about selling the Progress Brewing Company started near the time Oklahoma was debating repealing its prohibition laws. President E.I. Streich, Gustave's brother, announced the sale of the brewery to Lone Star Brewing Company of San Antonio, Texas, on October 2, 1959. With expansion plans in mind, Lone Star president Harry Jersig saw Oklahoma as a potential place for an economic boom. All brewing of Progress beer was immediately halted, and it would only brew Lone Star beer once new equipment was installed.

With the purchase finalized on November 21, an expansion of thirteen thousand square feet added new office space and modified the plant to triple its capacity. Plans of installing a beer garden feature to mimic the look of old-world Germany were introduced as well. Glass-lined fermenter tanks replaced the old wooden tanks and increased output to 120,000 barrels of beer per year. The full expansion cost nearly $500,000 and was to be completed in mid-1960. Larger office space, extra storage space and dock facilities, as well as a $10,000 automatic hop strainer, were also part of the additions. An interesting fact was documented that in the fiscal year of 1958–59, Oklahomans consumed 64,000 barrels of beer based on the barrel tax revenue.

Led by an experienced team, Lone Star felt that this was the best time to enter the Oklahoma market. Jack C. Freeman served as vice-president, general manager and brewmaster for the renovated plant. Its target was to introduce consumers to a "beverage of moderation," and it believed that its product would surpass and satisfy Progress beer drinkers. Another advantage to market its beer was that of regionality, citing a better product with a smaller footprint. Harry Jersig climbed the ranks of Lone Star to

A Handcrafted History

Harry Jersig inspects the Lone Star brewery in Oklahoma City, circa 1961. *Courtesy of Western History Collections, University of Oklahoma Libraries.*

become president in 1948 and instilled a philosophy that there should be no weak links, from creation to "the last swallow in the bottle."

The first bottles rolled out around March 1960, and about one year following, the first expansion came with a new bottling line valued at $500,000. Three hundred cans or bottles could be packaged each minute with the latest equipment. A new beer called Marques hit the market, leading to thirty-five new jobs in the Oklahoma City plant. Oklahomans must have really enjoyed the beer because another expansion came in July 1964, when the plant increased in size by 30 percent. General Manager Clyde Ingle stated on July 12, 1964, to the *Daily Oklahoman*, "I have no doubt that we will be needing another expansion of the plant next year." Sales and deliveries increased to 18 percent compared to 1963. Much of this was backed by the entry into the Arkansas market that was being handled by the Oklahoma City plant. In October 1965, a proposed $1 million expansion began the first phase of a four-story stock house. Other intentions were to house seven 680-barrel tanks for fermenting and storage. Increased production at the

Lone Star Brewery, 501 North Douglas, Oklahoma City, Oklahoma, September 15, 1960. *From the Ray Jacoby Collection, Oklahoma Historical Society Research Division.*

Oklahoma City plant doubled from 120,000 to 260,000 barrels a year and created twenty new jobs. The third and final expansion came in 1967, when new automated equipment boosted production to 350,000 barrels per year. However, midway through the year, a union strike led to a three-day shutdown, with workers seeking a wage increase and fringe benefits.

In January 1971, Lone Star declared that the Oklahoma City plant would close on March 15 due to economic circumstances. The past several years had not been profitable, and the brewery steadily lost its share of the market down to about 1 percent. Overall, pressure from national breweries and competition pushed the company to create a few ultra-premium beers. Yet, like many regional brewers at the time, numbers plummeted, and it lost out to the aggressive marketing campaigns from national brewers cutting into local markets. The six-story building was eventually sold and renovated for its current owner, Oklahoma League for the Blind. Lone Star Brewing Company of San Antonio was later acquired by a subsidiary of the Olympia Brewing Company in 1976.

A Handcrafted History

Drinking on Tulsa Time:
Ahrens Brewing Company (1938–1940)

Tulsa was founded along the Arkansas River by the Loachapokas and Creeks, creating Indian territory as a result of being driven from their original home in Alabama on the "Trail of Tears." Tulsa eventually grew into a small cattle rancher's town and was incorporated as a city in 1898. Three years later, oil was discovered, and a new industry drew in thousands of people to drill for the "black gold." Tulsa soon became the "Oil Capital of the World," housing about forty major and five hundred minor oil companies. Over time, Tulsa built up a sturdy infrastructure, and two brothers figured that it was time the city needed a brewery in the height of the "Golden Era."

Walter and George Ahrens started planning in 1934 to piece together a business plan and raise enough capital to start a small regional brewery. Predicated on their business plan, the brothers showed how significant the brewing industry was to raise generous amounts of tax revenue to the state, citing that between 1934 and 1935 the government took in more than $230 million. At the time, Tulsa had the highest buying power per capita of any city its size in the nation. There was certainly room to grow the market, as the per capita consumption was almost half of the pre-Prohibition numbers. Another argument for a local brewery was the lower cost of production as opposed to the competition being brought in by freight and marking up their products.

As operators of Southern Mill and Manufacturing Company, founded in 1919, the brothers were looking for a more profitable venture. More than $250,000 was invested to hire brewery engineer O. Frank Koenig, who had relocated to Tulsa for petroleum engineering. No high-grade revolutionary brewhouse was complete without a highly experienced brewmaster. Oscar S. Scholz came to the United States as a brewing consultant to many engineers and established brewmasters. Raised in Budweis, he graduated from the Royal Imperial Academy of Vienna. After graduating, he became the assistant director of brewery technology at the academy. He spent six years as a brewing specialist in the use of beer for medicinal purposes. Later, his career would span from brewing at Hull Brewery in England to the Budweiser-Budvar Brewery in Pilsen.

Construction moved swiftly starting in January 1938, with architect Leon Senter, and was completed ahead of schedule to the point that beer was filling vats as early as May. The plant boasted an initial capacity of 20,000 barrels of beer per year, with room to expand up to 100,000 barrels

Ahrens Brewing Company brewery exterior. *Courtesy of Sean Ahrens.*

when demands justified. Around 200 barrels of beer were brewed at a time utilizing hops imported from Europe and water sourced from the Spavinaw water system to help make its first product, Ranger Beer. "The people in Tulsa like their beer in as big a glass as they can find, and therefore Ranger must be mellow," described Oskar Scholz in an article from the *Tulsa World* on August 10, 1938. Ingredients were sourced from around the globe, from Pilsen- and Oregon-grown hops to European barley; the result was to brew a pale beer "that has a wonderful mellow taste…flavored with pleasant hops that will give it an unmistakable tang," claimed Scholz. Ranger Beer Week was declared in Tulsa on August 15 as the first batch of beer rolled out. Secretary-Treasurer George Ahrens declared, "We are dedicating this enterprise to the purpose of making a product of which every Tulsan may be proud. It is our sincere hope that Ranger Beer will merit the approval and patronage of those who find enjoyment in beer and that as demand for our product increases, gainful employment may be furnished to a constantly increasing number of Tulsans."

A small yet experienced team consisted of Walter Ahrens, who served as president; his brother as secretary-treasurer; C.F. Koenig as general manager; O.S. Scholz as brewmaster; and E.C. "Vic" Vickers as sales manager. The product was marketed with the slogan "The Zest of the West" and had a rich connection to a western cowboy theme. They also had their own baseball

A Handcrafted History

Above: Ranger Beer wooden beer crate. *Courtesy of The Downtowner LLC.*

Left: Ahrens Brewery Tulsa Tribune Ranger Beer ad. *Courtesy of Sean Ahrens.*

team, the Tulsa Rangers, to provide branding and sponsored a support group called the Rangerettes. A taproom was installed with the aesthetics of an outdoor beer garden, and guests could take a tour and sample the beer at the large wooden bar built by the mill workers.

With a brand-new brewery and trained staff to create a world-class beer for Tulsa, success seemed inevitable. Without much detail, the brewery only lasted just under two years and was forced to close on February 16, 1940. It is unclear if finances were too heavy early on or if taxation was too heavy-handed for them. Some rumors argue that local competition and "unfair" business practices from Oklahoma City–owned breweries had bullied them out of the market. To put an even more grim stain on history, Ahrens dumped 2,250 barrels of beer because it would have been too costly to make a $1,000 profit.

1959 Liquor Control Act

In April 1953, the Oklahoma House passed a vote 99-13 to hold a state election on the repeal of the 3.2 beer law in the 1954 general election. Other matters like local option and package sales were left for another time. After the Second World War and the proliferation of the new breweries established in Oklahoma, there was a new societal acceptance of beer. As George Nigh of McAlester stated in the *Daily Oklahoman* on April 1, 1954, so eloquently, "I don't want to go back to the times in my county when the folks of Krebs couldn't take a bath because the tubs were full of Choc beer." The tax revenue was more than enough incentive bringing in more than $5.9 million in beer taxes in 1952. A political fight ensued, and proponents, led by Dry United, raised a petition to put a county option beer question on the November general election ballot. In October 1957, a new coalition named Oklahoma United was formed to educate the public about the benefits of the brewing industry and its economic impact. "We have been remiss in permitting professional prohibitionists to present a distorted and frequently false picture without opposition," claimed Mark F. Dykema in the *Daily Oklahoman* on October 2, 1957; Dykema was then vice-president of Progress Brewing Company and president of Oklahoma United Committee.

Litigation between these two organizations tied up any advancement for two years. Finally, peace was struck to hold the county option election on December 3, 1957. Oklahoma United came out firing with a massive effort to sway the public from not repealing the 3.2 beer law. There were more than 11,000 employees of the beer industry and around 4,200 licenses issued in the state. Dykema argued the point in the *Daily Oklahoman* on October 2, 1957: "We don't have to change minds. We have to get the product users out to vote. Most of the products are bought by women, by the housewife for the home at the package store." Beer producers knew their market and even formed a women's organization to spread the word. This was a mission to educate the public that the local option was a terrible idea and that the tax revenue lost from beer sales would not easily be regained by a tax increase.

There was also a heated argument in the same article that the newly formed Christian League for Legal Control was a front for the beer industry, something Mr. Dykema vehemently denied. The league members declared themselves "liberal Christians who want legal control of liquor instead of bootleg control such as we have now." Its goal was to raise $500,000 to repeal constitutional prohibition in Oklahoma and support any candidate running for governor who agreed with its position. An illustrated ad run by the Oklahoma United Committee in November just weeks before the vote hit home by stating that a 50 percent tax increase was inevitable to make up the $11 million in tax revenue the beer industry created each year. One last tactic from the United Drys caught the organization passing around false literature that claimed whiskey would be licensed and the current Oklahoma prohibition law would be determined. Those were major topics that Mr. Dykema struck down fast. He reiterated that the fastest way to go back to bootlegging, Choc beer and homebrew was voting for the county option. The final result favored the Oklahoma United Committee, and the Oklahoma Alcoholic Beverages County Option Amendment, also known as state question 376, was defeated by the people.

Leading up to the governor's race, candidates debated licensing and taxing the sale of liquor. Many drys would uphold the laws; however, if a special election were called by a petition, they would not overlook it. George Miskovsky ran for the 1959 gubernatorial election on a compelling platform to repeal Oklahoma's prohibition laws and take back control from the bootlegging underworld. His claim was to tap the source already in use, which would amount to nearly $17 million per year to be placed in the general fund. He was defeated in the primary by J. Howard Edmundson, who handily became the sixteenth governor of Oklahoma in 1959. He took the reins of ending bootleg control and called for plugging loopholes in the state liquor control laws.

Edmundson went to work setting up four committees to discuss provisions for the repeal act. The result was a repeal plan set as an amendment to the constitution at a special election to vote on package store repeal without a county option, as well as a second election within two years on the question of county option. Thus began the arguments for and against. His plan also called for the formulation of a three-member Oklahoma alcoholic control board for strong beer. The board's initiative was to "provide strict regulation, control, licensing and taxation of the manufacture, sale, distribution, possession, and transportation of beer," as stated in the *Daily Oklahoman*. Open saloons would be prohibited, meaning no "liquor by the drink" or sale of alcohol on-premise. The new measure would limit the sale to original, sealed packages, prohibiting the sale on Sundays, holidays and election days. Most specifically, it provided a framework for the repeal of prohibition provisions of the constitution and went into effect once voted on by the people and the appointment of the new governor.

Naturally, many drys went before legislators to argue against repeal. Most represented the WCTU and local pastors, disputing the economic benefits and arguing that the morality of it would be in question. A repeal was the governor's top priority to be settled so the legislature could know if liquor taxes would be available to generate new revenue. Bootlegging was heating up as well, and local law enforcement was being taxed heavily trying to keep up as liquor came in via bus, automobile and plane. Edmundson hired a young Muskogee County lawyer by the name of Joe Cannon to enforce prohibition laws from January to March 1959. "Cannonball Joe" went on a mission to enforce prohibition so strictly that Oklahomans would vote for a controlled system. Kay Morgan from the *Oklahoman* wrote, "He grounded airplanes, raided bottle clubs, searched trucks on highways and earned the name 'Dracula' by asking that all auto accident fatality victims be given blood tests to determine if they had been drinking." On February 13, 1959, the Senate passed a measure calling for a special election on April 7, with uncertainty over whether there should be state-owned versus privately owned liquor stores. A poll indicated that 70 percent were for repeal, 56 percent were in favor of privately owned liquor stores and 53 percent were for local options. The measure was approved by an 81-37 vote that called for liquor sales in privately owned package stores and for two-thirds of tax revenue to go to the general fund. Oklahomans finally got to vote on the repeal of prohibition after fifty-one years—they had turned it down in five previous elections. The United Drys launched a statewide attack preaching on the radio the evils of alcohol, but this was swiftly countered by the United Oklahomans for Repeal, which educated the masses on a platform of control, arguing that people would obtain liquor legally.

A Handcrafted History

On April 7, 1959, Oklahoma voted 396,845 to 314,380 and passed House Bill 825, which allowed the sale of packaged liquors and finally repealed prohibition. Finally, on September 1, Edmundson issued a proclamation, and Oklahoma entered a new era of alcohol stronger than 3.2 percent ABW sold by a licensed retail package store at room temperature. Also repealed were 130 liquor statutes that had accumulated since statehood. One left untouched concerned drinking or being drunk in public. The bill also formed the ABLE commission (Alcohol Beverage Laws Enforcement). Governor Edmundson finally signed the Liquor Control Act into law on June 23. However, before that, the ABLE funds were slashed about 60 percent, cutting the spending from $500,000 to $235,000—a peculiarity then that has survived today, as the ABLE commission is run with minimal resources. Progress Brewing Company, the only brewery that remained in Oklahoma, filed for the first-ever manufacturer's license to brew 5.2 percent beer in the state—issued by the ABC board. Beer sold at wholesale for four dollars per case, just ten cents more than 3.2 beer.

ALL'S QUIET ON THE PLAINS, 1976-1992

When Oklahoma repealed prohibition, a part of the new legislation stated that no brewer, winery or distiller can enter into a franchise agreement with licensed liquor distributors in Oklahoma. In 1976, Oklahoma's distribution laws, commonly known as reverse franchising or the open wholesale system, prompted an Ardmore distributor to sue Coors for turning down an order because the brewing company already had a distributor in the same territory. An Oklahoma Supreme Court judge issued an opinion ruling that Coors violated Oklahoma's distribution laws. Coors decided then to pull all strong beer out of the state, and Anheuser-Busch along with Miller discontinued selling strong beer in Oklahoma in 1977. They continued to only sell the "non-intoxicating" 3.2 percent ABW beer since it was not regulated by ABLE and they could self-distribute the beer. The reasons behind this massive move was control over the quality of their products from production to the consumer. This wasn't possible with the current system, in which the product is "imported" by a wholesale distributor. When a distributor sells to a liquor store, they aren't required to follow the manufacturer's policies concerning their product.

An effort to amend the constitution was made in 1976 to allow liquor by the drink. A 1979 article from *Oklahoma* magazine detailed several facts that occurred. Tulsa supported the vote by 65.8 percent, while Oklahoma City only voted 54.5 percent due to the business community fearing repercussions from prominent drys in the city. The constitution banned open saloons and defined them as "any place, public or private, wherein the alcoholic beverage is sold or offered for sale, by the drink; or sold, offered for sale, or kept for sale, for consumption on the premises." Along with that was the warm beer section, where "No person shall deliver alcoholic beverages for retail sale except at ordinary room temperature." It was assumed that people were too tempted to drink their alcohol on the spot before taking it home. Finally, in a humorous issue related to dancing, no one could be served "non-intoxicating" beverages where private or public dancing was conducted. Many efforts to keep these laws in effect went to the wayside, and law enforcement could only shake down so many joints for serving illegally. In Tulsa, there were "clubs" where an adult could purchase a bar drink by purchasing a member card for a dollar.

Over time, it became exhausting and harkened back to days of bootlegging and backdoor dealings that were prevalent in early statehood and prohibition times. It was time Oklahoma stood up and regulated the liquor industry. Senator Bob Cullison took charge with his staff to author a bill in 1984 and usher in the Liquor by the Drink amendment. He received a lot of calls on the topic trying to appease "wholesalers, retailers, club owners, preachers, drys, hotels, and restaurants." Patterned loosely on Texas's laws, it took a page from Massachusetts with its happy hour laws. Dry counties wanted to be left alone and continue under the "liquor by the wink" system, which was free from taxes and control. Instead, Cullison wrote that bottle clubs could operate with hefty membership fees. So with that, on July 1, 1985, the law went into effect and Oklahoma woke up to a new era in how citizens socially interacted with alcohol. All of this was taken on by someone who started from scratch and poured most of a legislative year into creating the law. "It was difficult for me because I didn't know anything about the liquor industry and not much about liquor," said Cullison.

Citizens settled into the low-point beers that were specially brewed by the major brewing operations, known as BMC (Budweiser, Miller and Coors). It was a stagnant time for beer in the country, as the overall brewery numbers had dwindled to two digits compared to the thousands that were prolific in the pre-Prohibition era. With the "non-intoxicating" 3.2 beer law in place, Oklahoma was not a state where anyone could initiate growth in the business market. Culturally speaking, folks who had experienced high-quality, strong beer avoided the area or ventured to nearby states like Texas or Missouri to purchase stronger beer.

Such a drought led many folks to brew up their own beer. People from other cultures who immigrated to the United States or had traveled abroad were in search of the quaffable and rich flavors of beer they drank. Homebrewing has been a prevalent practice in this country and dates back to the Pilgrims who set up the first colonies. Over time, it has diminished due to the rise of breweries creating mass-produced alcoholic beverages and providing convenience to the people. The repeal of Prohibition mistakenly left off the legalization of making beer at home until Jimmy Carter signed H.R. 1337 on February 1, 1979, creating an exemption of taxation for homebrewed beer intended for personal consumption. Oklahoma eventually caught on some thirty-one years later and legalized homebrewing in 2010. Championed by homebrewer Gary Shellman and bill sponsor Representative Colby Schwartz, HB2348 was signed by Governor Brad Henry on May 11 and went into effect on August 26, 2010. Overall, it reclassified the previously required "license" as a "permit," which allowed the bill to include "transport to and use at organized affairs, exhibitions or competitions, including, but not limited to, homemaker contests, tastings or judgings." Those reasons were an incentive for a small group of Tulsa beer enthusiasts to form the Fellowship of Ale Makers in 1984. The group consisted of men and women who would come together and discuss beer, share what they made and give feedback. But it wasn't enough for some of those homebrewers and visionaries, and the only brewing took place at home until nearly eight years later.

BELLY UP TO THE BREWPUBS, 1992–2003

Bricktown Brewery (1992–Present)

There was a spark of entrepreneurialism when homebrewers shared their beers with friends and received accolades and suggestions to start a brewery. On the West Coast, people were doing just that as Jack McAuliffe started New Albion Brewing in 1978. As interests developed, more microbreweries fired up operations, like when "Buffalo" Bill Owens decided to leave his day job and created Buffalo Bill's Brewery after legislation allowed brewpubs in California around 1983. More consumers were drawn to the full-bodied, unpasteurized and additive-free beers. Watching the process live as patrons enjoyed a meal was a new and exciting experience one could only have found outside the country. The McLain family, who owned the city block from the railyard to Oklahoma Avenue in OKC, partnered with a restaurant group that embraced this new brewpub enterprise. Of course, Oklahoma law didn't allow for brewpubs to be a legal operation, so they took it upon themselves to go through the legal process of hiring a lobbyist and championing a new era of brewing in Oklahoma.

In April 1992, Governor David Walters signed legislation that would authorize a restaurant to brew beer. Representative Kevin Hutchcroft of Oklahoma City sponsored the legislation, which was approved by both houses. Oklahoma joined twenty-one other states to allow eateries to brew beer for on-site consumption. This did not change the "non-intoxicating" 3.2 ABW beer though. Light beers had been dominating the country throughout

Brewing vats arriving for the Bricktown Brewery, 1 North Oklahoma Avenue, August 25, 1992. *From the Journal Record Collection, Oklahoma Historical Society Research Division.*

the 1980s, and trying to craft a beer style that was meant to have a higher alcohol percentage was a challenge. It was only fitting that the site of Oklahoma's first brewery since Lone Star closed in 1976 was being erected in a pre-Prohibition building. Bryan Jester and Tom McLain, managing partners of Bricktown Brewery, envisioned the newest concept in Oklahoma as more than another restaurant. Nestled proudly on the corner of Oklahoma and Sheridan, the brewery was constructed inside a two-story warehouse originally built in 1903—the former home of a coffee roaster, wholesale grocery operation and candy warehouse. As it was one of three restaurants in the new four-block district known as Bricktown, the area wasn't quite a destination point for entertainment yet.

Brewing their own local beer added extra value for the customers, who viewed the giant copper and brass brewing vats behind glass and were educated about small-batch beers. As head brewer and a graduate of the University of California–Davis, humble homebrewer Luke DiMichele utilized his master's degree in fermentation and brewed the first legal craft beer in Oklahoma. An interesting note was that they used only natural ingredients, following traditional German purity laws known as the *Reinheitsgebot*. To ensure perfection of this new endeavor, the sixty-year veteran brewer Karl Strauss was brought on to help formulate the beer recipes. Bricktown at the time was building up more interest as a tourist attraction, and what better way to draw people in than with a new experience in an otherwise aging warehouse district? Guests had the option of five regionally named beers on tap: Land Run Lager, Bison Weizen, Red Brick Ale, Santa Fe Rail Ale and what quickly became the flagship beer (and most popular), the Copperhead Amber Ale.

Business boomed like a land run, with patrons rushing to try the new brews. As Oklahoma City grew and expanded, so did interest in the brewpub. Bricktown could barely keep up. Luckily, a new $267 million downtown redevelopment project in 1994, dubbed Metropolitan Area Projects (MAPS), led them to invest $1 million to expand the brewpub to quell those issues. The major improvements revitalized downtown

A Handcrafted History

Oklahoma City by adding a fifteen-thousand-seat baseball stadium and a twenty-thousand-seat sports arena. They hired Richard Bloch of Yui Bloch Designs, who helped design more than one hundred brewpubs to add 7,500 square feet of space and renovate the upstairs. It soon became a large sports pub with twenty-one deluxe billiard tables, darts and shuffleboard, along with bandstands for live music—all enclosed inside an interior with exposed brick and refurbished wood floors for a turn-of-the-century theme. The draw of a newly developed district brewed up events as well as outdoor concerts featuring huge names like Big Head Tom and the Monsters and the Dave Matthews Band. Live music became a staple on Tuesdays and Fridays in the early days, with heavily lauded performers like the Nixons, Live, Cross Canadian Ragweed, Creed and the Doobie Brothers.

Bricktown Brewery coaster from 1993. *Author's collection.*

Around the winter of 1995, the McLains expanded next door with an Italian-themed restaurant called Windy City. Naturally, it brewed a specialty beer called Fire Ale, a light-bodied red ale perfect for pairing with Chicago-style pizza and pasta. While it had a good run, the endeavor didn't last and saw several other incarnations. However, the current Bricktown group is planning on opening a new pizza parlor in the very same place soon, bringing the concept full circle. After a few years of instant success with the niche business model, the brewpub expanded to the upstairs, where a large stage was built for live music. A partnership with the Wynkoop Group expanded it even further into the adjacent buildings with a pool hall, an arcade and bar games. To draw in more regulars, the brewpub had a VIP Brew Club, which entitled members to food and beer discounts, a free shirt and billiards. More beers were added to the lineup, with ever-changing seasons and menu, like an altbier brewed with Munich malts and a spicy finish with Liberty hops or a Bavarian-style pilsner called Panhandle to beat the Oklahoma heat.

Good times were rolling as Bricktown became the area to hold festivals, like an annual Oktoberfest where 14 barrels of an Oktoberfest marzen were consumed in just ten days. National holidays like the Fourth of July and New Year's Eve were always big turnouts for fireworks, and St. Patrick's Day is still the largest party in downtown OKC and the Bricktown district—not to mention the annual Blues, Barbeque and Jazz festival.

By 1997, though, the honeymoon was over, and head brewer at the time Doug Moeller left to strike out on his own in Missouri. Beer production plummeted to 1,950 barrels in 1995 from 2,650 the year before. April 1998 saw the introduction of Miller products on tap to quell the requests of local patrons who wouldn't convert. Quality issues arose as well, and Jack Sparks, the brewer for the Interurban Brewpub groups, helped tweak the recipes and brewing techniques. He was retained for future consulting and worked alongside head brewer Mike Everly. "We took a look at the cleaning schedule that they were using and we decided to make a few changes," Jack reported to the *Southwest Brewing News*. "I honestly feel that in the next couple of months some of the finest beer in Oklahoma will be brewed here at Bricktown."

Like the winds sweeping down the plain, a shift in ownership swiftly came around 2001 when Jim Cowan, one of the original general managers, purchased the Bricktown Brewery from the McLain family. His other endeavor was a family-run business called Jake's Ribs in Chickasha. In 1999, you could get some authentic barbecue served alongside Bricktown beers and vice versa at Jake's. One shining achievement was a beer produced in 2004 brewed with local Oklahoma flavor called the Panhandler Wheat, which utilized red wheat harvested from the state's panhandle. More attractions were developed in the Bricktown district, like the water canal in 1999 and the Ford Center, which held major concerts and sporting events. At one point around 2004, Bricktown put Copperhead Ale in bottles thanks to a small group out of Kansas City. It was sold in Oklahoma liquor stores for a good year until that company went out of business and Bricktown discontinued bottling.

Bricktown made a good run of keeping the business afloat, but after seven years, Jim decided to turn it over to the current ownership, led by president Buck Warfield, formerly of the Rock Bottom brewpub chain. The first order of business was to bring back Charles Stout to run the daily operations. Charles was a manager from the very beginning, with a rich history in the Oklahoma restaurant business. He briefly left to work for the BJ's Restaurant and Brewpub chain but was given a massive opportunity to update Bricktown and reposition the whole business. An entire revamp of the menu took place by steering away from barbecue and back to traditional brewpub fare. Charles brought in industry professionals to give the brewery an overhaul, and with new head brewer Mark Carter, they redesigned and renamed the beers to keep up with modern trends in the craft beer industry. New life and energy were injected into the now sixteen-year-old brewpub, and the updated beers like Old King Kolsch and Blueberry Wheat are mainstays to this day, along with seasonal releases.

With new beer pumping through their vessels, the next step was expanding the brand past the walls. Charles recalled that a few naysayers opined that having a brewpub called Bricktown outside of OKC was crazy. "The first one was at Remington Park Casino and Racing Track. They wanted a partner to create a fun restaurant for their gamblers and luckily we had a good relationship with them already and were chosen," said Charles. The first standalone restaurant was in the little town of Shawnee, Oklahoma, and people embraced it from the beginning. As the years progressed, they opened in other major urban hubs like Owasso, Edmond, Tulsa and Midwest City. The real testament was being well received in Fort Smith, Arkansas, where they had a two-story facility that was similar to the old building they were founded in. "We went to the first one in Wichita and it was the same thing. People didn't realize Bricktown was an entertainment district in Oklahoma City, they just thought it was an interesting name for a brewery. We did really well there so we opened a second one," recalled Charles. Other areas included military cities like Lawton and one of their best-running restaurants in Springfield, Missouri. With so many locations sprouting up, there was obviously a need for more beer (except in Texas, where state laws prohibited Bricktown from selling its own beer). Around 2014, Bricktown struck a deal with Huebert's Brewing and contract-brewed its beers at that facility until 2019. Bricktown now utilizes the larger facilities in Krebs along with the shipping department to supply beer at all of its restaurant locations.

At present, the original facility brews mainly for itself, allowing for more unique beers and giving it a true taproom feeling. "We have more fun now with brewing some funky beers, firkins, and barrel-aged beers along with our core lineup," said Charles. Regarding the Bricktown story, he stated, "You have to note the alcohol restrictions we were given, with 3.2 beer we had gotten beat up and made fun of all those years because we couldn't brew strong beer. Then all of a sudden, session beer becomes popular and everyone starts saying it's not about the alcohol but the flavor, and by that time they switch the rules and we're now allowed to brew strong beer after 2016. All of our beers did go up in alcohol but only where appropriate for the style of beer."

All in all, Bricktown has stuck with its core values for the consumer all these years by offering local beer, great food and truly friendly service at each place you visit. "That's why every time I check in with one of our places

I test the beer to make sure we are keeping up with consistency," claimed Charles. What you'll see consistently at all of these sites is the emphasis on local beer being served on tap, even if it is not Bricktown. Charles noted, "We strive to be a truly friendly company and create relationships with our regulars and provide an environment where everyone is comfortable. Over time we got ahead of the game and asked for feedback on new menu items, or when a brewer is making a new beer he'll come out and let them sample a beer mid fermentation. Being a part of this community is really important, and I've been on the board of directors for the Bricktown Association and we all work together to promote Oklahoma City and promote good local craft beer."

CHERRY STREET BREWERY (1993–1996)

Known by many as a far-sighted innovator, Tom Ackley opened Cherry Street Brewery in December 1993 at the time when brewpubs were hot. He thoroughly worked up a business plan and schemed up a clever idea in March to raise funds for his new brewpub thanks to a new allowance by the Oklahoma Securities Commission for "small companies seeking to raise money." Led by Mark Icenogle, president of stock and bond broker Patterson Icenogle Inc., Tom grasped the opportunity: "This has all the positive aspects of doing business—the preservation of a historic property, working with quality people, we are dealing with something that does not hurt the environment, and this is a wonderful business opportunity." To raise the $1 million he needed to build out the fourteen-barrel brewhouse, Tom sold 200,000 shares of his company at $5 per share. It caught on like wildfire, to the point that some seven hundred locals invested in the idea of owning a piece of a brewery where they could take their friends and family. Shareholders owned just under 50 percent, with the remaining majority stake held by the operators.

However, the same genius and ego of this plan ultimately contributed to its demise. Tom became pretty inflexible about making changes through the buildout almost immediately. "The biggest challenge initially, aside from raising a million dollars, was the location on 15th and Peoria in the abrupt closing of Lincoln Elementary school. We were set up in the free-standing building back along the east boundary of that square block. That building was constructed before statehood, nothing was measured correctly, nothing was inspected, there was little to no plumbing and no political entity or

A Handcrafted History

Cherry Street Brewery building exterior development site. *Courtesy of James Ross.*

Cherry Street Brewery kitchen and brick oven buildout. *Courtesy of James Ross.*

Cherry Street Brewery's fermenters were installed on the second floor. *Courtesy of James Ross.*

inspector to come around to kick the tires every once in a while if you will," recounted James Ross, first general manager of Cherry Street Brewery, which was situated in Lincoln Plaza at 1516 South Quaker. Because of all these little hiccups, it delayed the process of building out such a new concept in a building so old that it almost needed to start from scratch. Meanwhile, Tom pumped up the crowds on his idea, selling stocks limited to a minimum of 100-share lots where the majority had 1,500 or less. Like anything when people invest, they want to see some results, and people grew rather impatient when an early July opening was pushed back to October and finally December.

In trying to sophisticate the beer market, Tom was up against many challenges in Oklahoma, especially with the squirrely 3.2 beer laws and a general population that really only knew of Bud, Miller and Coors. These light lagers were known as "lawnmower beers," drinks you could slam without thinking about it or what food you'd pair it with. National-scaled breweries dominated more than 90 percent of the market, especially in the Oklahoma grocery or convenience stores, where everything cold had to be 3.2 beer. "Was it a little bit ahead of its time? Sure. The Midwest can be a little slow in the tidal wave of change from either coast. Then I think to a certain extent Ackley and we all shot ourselves in the foot because we tried to be all things to everybody." said James. "My focus was to make the microbrewery and let that be the focal point. We sell beer. Tom wanted a full-scale restaurant upstairs, so then you're trying to manage that with a menu he wanted full control over, and then you put a brick-fired pizza oven in the pub downstairs. And the profit, we had twenty-five cents into every $1.25 beer we sold. So where were we going to make the money? Hustle and develop the beer."

Speaking of beer, the head brewer was Ike Manchester, who originated from the East Coast and was a fourth-generation sailmaker. Ike dug into his first brewing venture with only four batches of homebrew under his belt and quickly became an assistant brewer in California. To hone his craft, he attended the Siebel Institute of Technology in Chicago and graduated in November 1992. A consulting job in Florida led to Tom Ackley inviting Ike for an interview. "The opportunity to be involved from the ground up

Cherry Street Brewery fermenters behind glass. *Courtesy of James Ross.*

piques the interest, to say the least," Manchester told the *Tulsa World*. He would go on to brew beers with regional names like Lincoln Lager, a Munich helles that consisted of Perle, Hallertauer and Spalt German hops and is lagered for two months; Red Bud Amber; Scissortail Pale Ale; Bullseye ESB; Blackboard Bitter; and Skyline Porter. "They treated the brewery as the main source and drawing card to the restaurant," Manchester said.

With the restaurant spinning too many plates, the food suffered, and when that happened the brewpub started to get a bad reputation. Eventually, that trickled down to people not wanting to patronize the place and who resisted trying the new beers being brewed. "At the time we had a flight of 6 beers for a song back then and nobody wanted to try them!" exclaimed Jim. Another key example of bleeding money early was the exorbitant labor costs from the kitchen staff, who would do prep work overnight. As times got harder, walls were built up and communication dwindled between Tom and his staff. It appeared that he couldn't delegate the tasks to those he hired. Again, it was trying to go big all at once instead of building up a following with the beer, which had the best profit margin, and sticking to the wood-fired pizza oven in the pub would have been minimal for operating costs. "If we had a dance floor upstairs and live music we'd have made a killing. And you can go until midnight or two depending on the noise level and everyone drinking your beer, but that's just my opinion," claimed Jim. As mentioned, there was a generational gap that eventually closed around the late 2000s in Tulsa with new bars and restaurants catering to a young professional crowd. No-expense-spared gimmicks—from a name-your-own-beer contest to complex etched crystal glassware that exploded every time you wash them and even a brick pavers program for the shareholders—fed the death of it. After talking to Jim further and learning about Ackley's first endeavor at the 15th Street Grill, a fine dining establishment, it could be argued that some of those concepts made their way over to the brewpub—naturally, they did not fit the atmosphere.

About eight months after opening, ownership changed hands to Terry Turner, another local restaurateur known for the French Hen in Tulsa. There was a transfer of stock to SRT Partnership, and in a press release, Tom claimed that the move was "a terrific opportunity for the brewery and its stockholders. It will maximize the potential of Tulsa's original community-owned brewpub." Turner and his group were looking to enhance the menu and improve food service, adding value to what was already in place. Their new head brewer, Chris Cauthon, started out with

A Handcrafted History

Cherry Street brewmaster Ike Manchester inspects the newly built brewhouse. *Courtesy of James Ross.*

a cherry beer called Orchard Ale that was fermented with cherry puree. Other beers featured in the fall of 1995 included a Vienna lager named Hildebrau; Polar Bear Pilsner, a light lager with Czech Saaz hops; Red Bud Amber; Prairie Pale Ale; Weewoka Wheat, an unfiltered American wheat ale; Swan Lake Light, which appealed to the light beer drinkers and was brewed with an organic hop; Pride of Ringwood and Fuggles; and Good Gus Stout. Chris placed tenth in the Great American Beer Festival for his Molly Brown Ale, a low-carbonated ale with a lot of chocolate malt and Willamette for the late hop addition. In the summer of 1996, all the effort at salvaging was too much, and the U.S. Bankruptcy Court for the Northern District of Oklahoma approved the $150,000 sale as part of the Chapter 11 reorganization by Cherry Street Brewery. The brewing equipment was sold to a California company for use in a microbrewery. The location transformed several times over, housing bars like the Slow Duck Saloon, the Gray Snail and its most current resident, Nola's, a Cajun restaurant. It was last reported that Tom moved to Costa Rica and set up a bed-and-breakfast, residing there to this day.

Interurban Restaurant & Brewpubs/Tulsa Brewing Company (1993–1998)

Not more than ninety minutes north up I-44, there was a restaurateur eyeing the success of this budding brewpub industry. Kenny Tolbert, a Broken Arrow High graduate and former oil businessman, ventured into the restaurant business, opening two Hoffbrau Bar and Grill locations in Tulsa. Kenny had a vision and teamed up with Interurban Restaurant owners Rusty Loeffler and Robert Ross to create their own brewpub, Tulsa Brewing Company. Taking the formula of success from both restaurants and adding a niche new spin of house-made draft beer was a brave endeavor for the small town. "The menu will be upscale. It's not what I call bar food. The intention is to make it where the customer does not feel like he is in a bar," Kenny relayed to the *Tulsa Business Journal* in July 1993.

The real focus was on the beer, and finding a top grade brewmaster was key in brewing to the specifications of Tulsans' taste and to the 3.2 law. Such was found with veteran brewmaster and consultant Mike Brotzman of Denver. Brotzman eventually met up with a local homebrewer named Mike Groshong, who shared a love of the outdoors and climbing. Groshong was elated to talk with a real brewmaster and over time shared his homebrews after a long day of rock climbing and mountain biking. The friendship continued as the buildout of Tulsa Brewing Company was slated for an opening in late July/early August. Brotzman was impressed with Mike's skills and invited him to brew his first batch of beer on a large scale. "I was hooked. I was like, OK, this is what I wanna do. I have a direction now. So he hired me after I learned all the systems and would be named brewmaster eventually," recalled Groshong. After about nine months, the brewpub was a huge success, with live music on the weekends and the parking lot continuously full; Mike recollected that "the tanks used to rock back and forth; you could see the beer going because there was so much being poured from the tap towers at one time it was causing them to shake."

Brewing for the low-point beer mandate meant procuring high-quality ingredients and better techniques to increase the flavor profile but not the alcohol. "At the time I wanted to brew beer compared to what you could find in Europe or at the liquor store. It was hard to find many unique styles in Oklahoma at the time," said Mike, referring to the selection of beer among a "lager ocean." Many of the initial brews were named after events, places and times in Oklahoma history. Some examples were Tornado Alley Porter, Route 66 Amber Ale, Porter Peach, Osage Wheat Ale, Honey Blond Light

A Handcrafted History

Craig Baxter, general manager of Tulsa Brewing Company, draws a Honey Blonde Light Pale Ale at the Tulsa Brewing Company near Seventy-First and Memorial on January 31, 1997. *Photo by Tom Gilbert.*

Pale Ale and other seasonal brews. Another aspect involved utilizing the beer for marinades, soups and sauces to create unique dishes only found there. The partners were banking on the popularity of the brewpubs in the country with a success ratio of nine out of ten compared to one out of ten for new restaurants. Large copper and steel brewing tanks were housed behind glass in the 7,900-square-foot building that was home to a previous Interurban location. The menu was cherry-picked from the other restaurants, offering only the highest-quality dishes.

Tulsa Brewing Company employed more than one hundred people, which included counsel from Dr. Michael Lewis, a brewing consultant and an educator from UC–Davis. Their goal was to focus on the community spirit and camaraderie around the appreciation for a quality tasting beer. "Then you've created what in England is called the public house, the neighborhood pub," Lewis reported to the *Tulsa World*. "There's a lot of *bon ami*, friendship, and warmth—you know each other." They led by example with a grand opening invitation-only event benefiting the Family & Children's Service Inc. It was nothing Tulsa or the state of Oklahoma ever had access to with the restaurant industry, and success took off fast. Iconic to what evolved today, people would ask how you pair a beer to food and always wanted to know what was on deck. Another in-house favorite was the Ugly Mug root beer made on site. The Tulsa Brews & Blues Festival was introduced in September 1995, bringing together a community of homebrewers, Fellowship of Oklahoma Ale Makers and major brewers in the nation. It was the first of its kind, with live music and a homebrew competition in which John Powers brewed the winning beer, which was later served at Tulsa

Brewing Company. In 1996, the festival was rebranded as Tulsa Brewfest with a smaller band and more beer. "This time we backed off the music and decided to feature the beer angle a little more," said Rick Bahlinger, organizer and marketing director for local contracted beer T. Paul's Beer. Beers from Oklahoma's brewpubs, regional microbrews, domestic breweries, imports and microbrews from large American brewers were featured. Most notable of the time were the T-Towne Red and T-Towne Lager, as well as Redding Golden Ale from Barleyfield Brewing Company.

Meanwhile, Mike brewed for three days in Tulsa and then commuted to Dallas to help build out a spin-off of Interurban that was Two Rows Brewpub. Texas had changed the brewpub laws in 1994, and the partners saw an untapped market that was rapidly growing. "They had left the framework of this building but all the walls were gone and wires hanging from the kitchen ceiling. It was just a mess. Then we got our equipment and management said in two weeks we'll be open so we need a beer. Grain bags were all over

Jeff Swearengin, assistant brewmaster of Tulsa Brewing Company; Mike Groshong, brewmaster; and Krystal Plyler, who is working on filling beer orders during Tulsa's Brews & Blues festival near Main Street and Brady in the Brady Arts District on June 7, 1997. *Photo by Tom Gilbert.*

Norman Brewing Company coaster. *Author's collection.*

the restaurant and we were sleeping there with three brewers making beer four days in a row until all the fermenting tanks were full. That was the first time I brewed a barleywine on a 30-barrel system; it was called Titanic Barleywine," recalled Mike. Dave Bracken performed brewmaster duties in 1995 to brew at Interurban Restaurant and Brewery in Norman and over another venture that was being built out at 50 Penn Square that would eventually break off and become Belle Isle Brewpub. Eventually, Randy Palmer relieved Dave, who went to brew in South Carolina. Randy stayed on at Interurban of Norman until the fall of 1996, at which time he found greener pastures in Houston and brewed at Two Rows Brewpub.

After a year of high success, it was time to expand. "Our intent has always been to expand," reported Tolbert to the *Tulsa World* in April 1994. The original Interurban restaurant in Norman, founded in 1976, received an upgrade with a joint venture between the three restaurateurs and the sixth brewpub in the state. Mike Brotzman left TBC to become the brewmaster for Interurban Restaurant and Brew Pub, which opened on June 9 at 105 West Main in Norman. "Renovations will include enclosing the former outside patio in glass, building a new outside patio, and expanding the bar. The charm of the old building will be retained by using glass, copper, stainless steel, and the original brick for an old industrial atmosphere," according to the press release. Managing partner Robert Ross highlighted, "We have really been pleased with the operation of Tulsa Brewing Co. We feel like the brewpub, with fresh beer served on the premises, is a good concept with good value." The cost of the new buildout was around $600,000, which added about two thousand square feet in brewery space. Renovation adhered to a turn-of-the-century motif to maintain the integrity of the former 1917 Norman Trolley Station it occupied. At this time, the Canadian River Limited Partnership transitioned to doing business as Interurban Restaurant & Brewpub. Canadian formed in January 1994 and acquired the assets of Interurban's former parent company, Oklahoma Foodservice Investments Inc. Rusty Loeffler served as president of Canadian while Ross served as vice-president. Kenny Tolbert and Mike Brotzman were joint venture partners. Brotzman eventually helped set up both brewpubs in Texas and helped build out the third sister brewery in Oklahoma City at 50 Penn Square Mall.

Back in Tulsa, Mike continued to create beers he loved like the Grumpy Stout and a collaborative beer from homebrewer David Moos called Brown Cow. In 1996, they held several four- to five-course Brewmaster's Dinner events, prepared by Chef Todd Dunn. He also teamed up with fellow Tulsan and avid homebrewer Jeff Swearengin to make a hefeweizen for the summer of 1997. Jeff, a medal-winning homebrewer, lent a wealth of brewing knowledge and skill to the place and became assistant brewer. To keep pace with summer drinkers, double-batch brew days were the norm back then, with Uncle Red's Razzberry Ale made with real raspberries. Other seasonal styles brewed included an Oktoberfest lager, a spiced pumpkin ale and an Okie IPA that was aged in pine casks.

Dave Bracken came on as a brewer for Interurban Brewpub in Norman and was originally slated to take on responsibilities for the third sister brewery. He only lasted a few months before being drafted by a South Carolina brewery; Randy Palmer, an assistant brewer at the time, stepped up. Palmer was tasked with brewing a blueberry ale; Box Car Bitter, a hopped-up ESB-style ale; Buck McPhail's Red Ale, named after an Oklahoma University football star; and a Mistletoe Oatmeal Stout. "Sales are going up," shared Randy, in a *Southwest Brewing News* column. "People are starting to get into the whole aspect of good beer. I've seen a lot of women drinking darker beers." Those included his Pecan Nut Brown, Barking Fish Porter and seasonal brews such as a spiced pumpkin ale, with one hundred pounds of pumpkin meat. Lighter beer styles included the ever-popular Osage Golden Wheat and later a California Common. In the later part of 1995, a legislative change allowed brewpubs to keg and sell their beer within the company. This led Oklahoma City IU Sports Grill to sell its beer without being a licensed brewpub.

By the end of 1996, Randy had left for Two Rows in Dallas and turned the reins over to Jack Sparks, who was also brewing for Belle Isle, the third sister brewpub. Jack left brewing in the middle of 1998, fed up with the arcane beer laws, and went to brew for Big Horn Brewing in Arlington, Texas. According to a column in the *Southwest Brewing News*, the High Plains Draughters homebrewers club claimed that Jack had a lot of firsts in Oklahoma brewing: "He brewed the state's first lager (an Oktoberfest); first multi-pub brewer; first distributorship; finally first to use mash tun as a hot tub." Near the end of 1998, Jack won a silver medal for his Addison Pale Ale at the Great American Beer Festival. He immediately turned in his resignation and served as a consultant for Bricktown Brewery while looking for a more full-time position. "I'm a bartender trained as a brewer

A Handcrafted History

Assistant Brewer Jeff Swearengin stirs the wort at Tulsa Brewing Company. *Courtesy of Jeff Swearengin.*

who happened to learn the craft and hobby of brewing in what I feel is the correct way on the job in the brewhouse from someone who also learned to brew the same way. One learns a hell of a lot more this way than at a damn brewing school," he told *Southwest Brewing News*. It was a telling sign of demise, as Interurban had ceased brewing operations in the middle of 1998 and sold off its brewing equipment to its neighbors at Coaches.

TBC stopped brewing beer on November 8, 1998, due to myriad issues among management as well as financial reasons, after suffering abysmal sales in October ($29,000) and losing two general managers in less than a year, on top of the fact that it let assistant brewer Jeff Swearengin go for no reason. A major budget cut eliminated live bands plus its license fee, lunch service was cut and advertising was practically nonexistent. To really go out with a bang, management raised the price of beer to $3.25 on the last two days it was open. "I really enjoyed brewing for Tulsa and the surrounding area," said Mike Groshong, TBC's brewmaster for more than five years. "I want to thank everybody for the greatest time of my life," he told Matt Alcott of the *Tulsa World*. Seventy-First Street in Tulsa was ramping up major chain restaurants focused more on food quality and not bars. "We were selling enough beer—around 1,200 barrels last year—it's just the restaurant side that had taken a hit over the last couple of months," said Groshong.

Belle Isle Brewing Company (1995–Present)

Penn Square Mall resides near the former site of Belle Isle, a water oasis formed in the early 1920s that generated power to streetcars that would operate down the middle of Classen Boulevard. Eventually, an amusement park was built with dancing pavilions and canoe rides, and it even hosted the Great Houdini, who performed an escape act. Close to the depression era, it had closed with the sale to Oklahoma Gas & Electric Company. The brewpub model was doing well enough with the Interurban ownership that they expanded into Oklahoma City. The original site housed a restaurant that was started in the late 1970s by the name of Pistachio's Restaurant and Bar and ran for about five years. Interurban moved in and took residence for eight years until Neill Hardin and David Reisenberg, restaurateurs with more than forty years of experience, broke away from the franchise to strike out on their own. They purchased the restaurant, the Urban Market and Interurban Catering. Originally, it was supposed to be David and Neill along with Rusty and Robert, but the latter two decided that they had enough debt

Belle Isle front entrance. *Photo by the author.*

and stayed on as a management team. "When we were trying to come up with a name for this when we bought it from Interurban, Neill and I along with the building managers were sitting at our bar during a happy hour for a brainstorming session. The area we are in is known as Belle Isle and the lake had a good history; plus it was consistent with Interurban because of the trolley system being powered by the original power plant where Wal-Mart now resides," stated David.

The beer was still brewed by IU, and they shared a common business model with similar menus and more than fifty beer recipes among the three, while each brewmaster put his own spin on them. Equipment wasn't cheap when the brewpub fad started. "Our brewhouse came from a company called PUB out of New Jersey that we had shipped here during the first brewpub boom when they were gaining popularity all over the country in the early 1990s. So we ordered it, put down all the money and it was six months behind schedule of us actually receiving it. We had to stop construction of the surrounding walls in the building in order to install the equipment," David recalled. Just like the explosion of a firework, the brewpub boom fizzled fast, with places closing left and right with expensive learning curves. Looking back, David reflected that not long after they opened, equipment flooded the market for sheet metal prices; had they waited, they could have gotten everything for ten cents on the dollar.

These lessons affected not only the owners but also patrons, as many of their taste buds were not aware of the styles Belle Isle brewed. "Our original brewer, Jack Sparks, brewed at Interurban as well but we paid him. Our second brewer, when he left, trained an employee that had never brewed before by the name of Mike Eberle," said David. Over time, Mike improved his skills, making crowd-pleasing beer, but then an offer to move to Durango, Colorado, was too good to refuse. "Mike was making a bottling line for us in between his time in Colorado. Sadly he was tragically killed in a car accident and put a big damper on the project and we never pursued bottling after that." Neill took up the helm after learning much from Mike and continued his education with several apprentice brewers who were employed early on. "They taught us quite a few things; one guy was a professor at OCU named Tony Stancampiano, and one of the best homebrewers I knew. He now works part-time with Stonecloud Brewing." Since then, all brewing duties have rested on Neill's shoulders for more than twenty years. "Brewpubs had become a trend like quiche in the early 1970s," Hardin told Paula Burkes of the *Oklahoman*. "I like physical work, and producing end-products people like." When they first opened, the Honey Blonde Ale was the only constant beer kept from all Interurban locations but went by the name Belle Isle Blonde. However, the other beer names are deeply rooted in the local history, patrons and family involved with the brewery.

In those early months, brewer Jack Sparks relayed to the *Southwest Brewing News*, "We're selling a lot more beer than anticipated." On any given day, you would smell the sweet wort wafting throughout the building when they first fired up the brew kettles. It was so distracting that the building security said they had to stop immediately. Well, naturally that doesn't just happen in the brewing process. Brew days consisted of 2:00 a.m. start times in the early days. Adhering to the low-point laws, the brewpub formulated some recipes you'd normally see tip the alcohol scale. One such beer was the roasty oatmeal stout, as Jack detailed the brewery's lineup:

> *I used 50 pounds of roasted malts and you could smell it across the room. When I brewed it people were coming to see it, they thought it smelled so good. We started out with five beers along with the blonde ale; an amber ale*

A Handcrafted History

Neill Hardin, the brewmaster at Belle Isle Restaurant & Brewing Company in Oklahoma City, March 12, 2009. *From the* Oklahoman.

>*named Flanagan's after an FBI agent that worked in the building; Power Plant Porter; Wild Mary Wheat, an American wheat ale; and Liberty Belle, a hefeweizen. Our seasonal beers include a peach ale, raspberry wheat and the rotating stout called Power Plant that fluctuated between an oatmeal stout and a porter; an Oktoberfest lager, our first lager in October of 1997, a California Common; an IPA that featured "shovels full" of Cascade hops; a Bulldog brown ale and a spiced up Winterfest with cloves and nutmeg.*

The two-story building was certainly a challenge to convert into a full-scale brewing operation, as David recalled. The fermenters and serving room were housed on the upper level, along with a stage for live music, billiard tables and a full bar. "When we originally opened you could see up into the brewpub from the bar down below. We thought we'd make it a two-story concept with the live music and billiards upstairs and full dining down below. Then we started having problems where it got too noisy for the downstairs diners, and every now and then a pool ball would come down into the bar below. So we concluded we spent $30,000 opening the hole and $60,000 covering it up," recounted David. "We should have shut down half a dozen times. We had a fire in 2002 that almost killed us. Five landlords and countless building managers." After they opened for business in 1995, the Oklahoma City Bombing really put a damper on it. Despite their downfalls, Belle Isle survived the first wave and in David's opinion has made it to the second as brewery models changed and adapted to the world. "When Interurban first opened, we only served our beers. We thought everyone else was the competition. But when we opened up Belle Isle, we thought, why would we tell our customers if you like Budweiser, we don't want you? So we started carrying everything, and it's been good for us. Those places brewed long before us and created the consumer's palate, and so we think you're sending the wrong image by only carrying your own beer."

Brewer and co-owner Neill Hardin kept busy with demand increasing every year. He hired Chuck Deveney, owner of the Brew Shop, in the summer of 2005 as an assistant brewer. Recipes were improved, with adjustments made to their popular El Diablo Ale with two-row wheat and Munich malts along with several additions of Mount Hood hops. They also devised an oatmeal stout that became a staple every March for St. Patrick's Day. In the summer of 2011, the brewpub went through a large remodel that doubled the size of the brewery. Seasonal beers continued to spring up over the years, like the crowd favorite Razzberry Wheat, which was introduced at the Paseo Arts Festival in Oklahoma City. Neill continues to craft their original lineup to complement an eclectic Americana menu and wood-fired pizzas.

Norman Brewing Company/Coach's/The Brewhouse (1993–Present)

The United Kingdom has served as a leader in classic beer styles and influenced many American brewers when they first started out. On one occasion, a political science student entered the basement of a pub one day to "study," placed a pound on the counter and pointed to the nearest handle of the beer engine. After contemplating his decision, he quaffed down a generous helping of cask ale, and his life was altered for good. Brian Smittle returned home, changed his major to a business degree and made his way to Vail, Colorado, with an itch to brew. He volunteered with a brewer he met up with at a beer festival the day before and saw the reality of brewing as a career unfold before him. While living with his sister, he became an avid homebrewer after his girlfriend gifted him a brewing kit. With that, he hunkered down and was employed to brew at Hubcap Brewery and Kitchen in Vail during the ski seasons from 1991 to 1993. Skiing during the day and brewing at night was the ultimate paradise for Brian. Near the end of the 1993 ski season, he gave a tour to two investors from Oklahoma, Chris Becker and Todd Reed, who wanted to expand the widely booming brewpub scene in Norman. A week later, he was given a plane ticket to come to look at the property proposed to house a new Specific Mechanical Systems brewhouse. Once the ski season concluded, he cut a deal to become a partner; moved to Norman, Oklahoma; and started the renovation of what would become the Norman Brewing Company.

Opening in December 1993, the eight-thousand-square-foot restaurant reinvented part of the famous DenCo Café in Norman that was under the ownership of Jack Hooper. Midway through 1994, there was a large expansion costing some $540,000. Red brick and timber were the main motifs, as twenty-two billiard tables filled the seven-thousand-square-foot buildout. The best update was the addition of four 350-gallon (ten-barrel) fermenting tanks to the brewery. Brian created a flavorful variety of beers, from a raspberry ale that utilized ten pounds of raspberries per barrel to the Funky Dunky dunkelweizen, built with 60 percent wheat and 40 percent Munich malts that were fermented using a yeast borrowed from Royal Bavaria, and special holiday ale brewed with cinnamon, ginger, nutmeg and orange peel. He expanded his portfolio with an ESB brewed with 100 percent British malt and his own proprietary British yeast and hopped with Kent Goldings. With an eclectic menu of buffalo steaks and quinoa salads, the concept seemed a bit ahead of its time.

To resonate better with the local college town crowd, the brewpub gained new partners in Hal Smith and Steve Owens and rebranded as Coach's Brewpub. The atmosphere was set for the college game-day crowd, with tailgate fare like pizza, BBQ and wings and screening local sports on four large fifty-four-inch TVs that formed one giant screen. The lineup of beers consisted of Sunset Light Ale, Harvester Wheat, Railyard Amber, Downtown Brown, Main Street Steam and the local favorite, Sooner Stout. Some seasonal beers were included like the Winter Ale and an IPA with a two-week dry hop addition. They also supplied fans a shuttle bus service to and from the University of Oklahoma Sooner football games. Brewing became quite a chore to keep up with other venues when they added Coach's BBQ and Brewery, so they added an assistant brewer named Matt Ehinger. Mike Groshong was hired a few years after Tulsa Brewing Company closed down. Matt finished his college degree and eventually moved to Dallas, where he now owns and brews at Bitter Sisters Brewing Company.

In the summer of 1998, negotiations between Coach's and Bricktown Brewery ownership broached the possibility of a merger. Brian Smittle confirmed by saying, "We have been in contact with the owners of Bricktown Brewery for several months now. The price and terms of the agreement were reached, but minor details concerning common maintenance at the building shared by Bricktown, Windy City, another restaurant, and some business offices will have to be worked out." Eventually, the deal fell through on the last day, but it was important to note as Bricktown ownership would change hands in the near future. In the spring of 1999, Coach's signed a lease with the brand-new Bricktown Ballpark that brought Triple-A baseball to Oklahoma and became its second location in Oklahoma City. "We signed a six-year lease," Smittle told the *Southwest Brewing News*. "The space is over 10,000 square feet and has two patios that overlook both left field and the new water canal. We have options to renew the lease for up to 16 years. We will upgrade the brewery in Norman to a 25 bbl system to handle the increase in production that this new adventure will create. We also ordered three additional storage tanks, a kegging machine, and 80 new kegs. We will serve four of our beers at first then expand to around eight taps. Thirty-two beers total will be on tap as well as our famous barbecue." The franchise also looked into the old Tulsa Brewing joint, and "we went so far as to actually put a few things down on paper. Someone could move in there for around $100,000 and be up and running brewing equipment and all in no time. We looked into it, but chose to pass," said Brian. At this point, they were also brewing two specialty beers for The Library in Norman, which boasted a tap system that was installed with help from Boulevard Brewing in Kansas City. A Tulsa location was finally put in around 2001 just down the street from the former Tulsa Brewing Company.

After almost a year at the ballpark, they were looking for a new system to keep up with brewing production. The thirty-barrel Specific System was installed in early 2003 and produced about one thousand gallons of beer at a time in the brew kettle. Plans for an Edmond location were underway in 2003 that offered all of Coach's beers along with several import taps. At the time, they were brewing for four locations in the state: Bricktown Ballpark, Okie Doke BBQ, Coach's Edmond and the Library Bar, where a special amber beer and an IPA aptly named the Library Ale was brewed especially for the thirty-five-tap draft house. However, with the new system down for three weeks to be installed and launched, there was quite a drought for beer in that time frame. As another staple, two beer trailers were set up at the tailgate tents during University of Oklahoma Sooner game days.

A Handcrafted History

High Country Hefeweizen was a popular beer that sold out fast until they upgraded their system. The IPA was slowly catching on as a year-round beer. One person of note was bartender turned manager and now professional brewer Jake Keyes, who wasn't an IPA fan. "I remember there was a group of regulars that walked over every day for happy hour and the oldest fellow in the crew was known as the Mayor of Coach's. They'd drink the IPA like it was a cult following. I could never drink it because I always felt it was too bitter. One day the mayor told me, 'Get yourself a growler when you finish your shift; shoot some pool, and force it down and tell me what you think.' I did it that day and I finished the growler and went right back to the bar and filled it up again and was hooked on IPAs ever since."

The ownership was also looking at other places to expand the celebrity/sports/BBQ–themed brewpub. Among all the great success and shattering sales records each year, there was a transition around the summer of 2006. Eateries Inc.—which owned Garfield's, Garcia's and Pepperoni Grill—acquired all three of the Coach's franchise stores. The brewery in Norman was shifted to where the pool hall was and rebranded as the Brewhouse, which continues operations to this day. Brian Smittle stayed on as general manager, and Mike Groshong continued to serve as brewmaster. With the acquisition, the new owners weren't quite as interested in the handcrafted beer business as Brian was. He stayed on for a few more years, brewing beer under the name Coach's, and supplied all of the locations with beer. Around the summer of 2008, the city of Austin pulled Brian and his family down to start his own endeavor with the creation of Thirsty Planet Brewing Company. "We poured the slab for the foundation on my birthday in the summer of 2009 and got the first beers out the door on June 30, 2010." Brian found a community to grow and expand in with a large thirty-barrel system and poignantly stated to the video series *The Beer Diaries*, "When you have a friend come in town to reconnect with, you don't do it over a glass of milk. You go out and grab a beer together."

The Brewhouse remains open today with the same business model and slightly modified beer recipes to reflect the alcohol reform changes allowing brewpubs to brew full-strength beer. "We took our flagship beers and we reimagined the recipes pursuing ABVs that we think are more in line with what people are interested in from their craft beer," said owner John Howell, thanks to the work of brewmaster Benjamin Rickman. It was licensed as the second brewery in the state, and there is a lot of history in the tanks at the Brewhouse, with its flagship wheat, amber and 80-day IPA. A stout has been brewed seasonally in smaller ten-barrel batches.

Royal Bavaria (1994–Present)

Many folks who think of retirement probably envision goals of relaxing with a hobby, traveling or settling down with their family. Jorg Kuhne had wrapped all of those ideas of retirement together and relocated in 1993 to Oklahoma, where his wife grew up. His vision was to own a German-inspired restaurant and brewery. Not exactly a picturesque idea of relaxing, to say the least. His intention was to develop an isolated place where people could experience old-world Germany with a traditional meal. Jorg wanted a location between Oklahoma City and Norman that served as a destination place, which is why he chose an area in the middle of an open field. "He actually chose this location by airplane," recalled Executive Chef Andy Gmeiner. Trained in Germany, with an impressive résumé of BA/master's degrees in culinary arts, a BA in restaurant management and a teacher's degree in culinary arts, Andy arrived in 1994 as a consultant for the buildout of the 5,200-square-foot restaurant and brewery. Working at five-star restaurants and a chain restaurant and cooking for booths at Germany's Oktoberfest gave him a large range of experience. Originally, he was only supposed to stay for six months to help build out the restaurant, but he stayed for a few years to build his knowledge of how American restaurants are run: "I wanted to see how they operate no matter if they were corporate or privately owned. I wanted to broaden my horizons and learn about them and apply it to Royal Bavaria. I had some consulting jobs with high-end steakhouses to smaller jobs and learned what the American public looks for when they dine out and learn different management styles." After Jorg finally decided to officially retire, Andy took over ownership in December 2007. "We don't allow any televisions here at the restaurant. Our goal is for families to have a conversation and enjoy an evening out," said Andy.

Once the plans were drawn up, Jorg employed the service of a company named Kaltenberg, owned by Prince Luitpold of Bavaria. Showcased behind large walls of glass stood the German-assembled brewery, with shiny copper kettles handmade in Germany used for brewing up to twenty-five thousand gallons of beer in the *Reinheitsgebot* tradition. An open fermentation method was originally incorporated that boosted the esters, elemental flavors in a beer typically found in traditional Bavarian-style beers. It is almost categorized as a natural product, with no pasteurization or preservatives, and it is about as fresh as you can get since the brewery only served its beer in house. The determining factor of freshness was the quality of foam, according to Jorg. "The stiffer the foam, the fresher the beer. It would be an insult in Germany to serve a beer without a head," Jorg told *Oklahoma Today* magazine. Another local Bavarian from Freilassing, Bernholdt Kuhn, was the brewery engineer contracted to brew and train Jorg, Andy and a local employee, Roger Steely, how to brew the royal beer and operate the brewery. Bernie, as he was known, brewed for the large Kaltenberg firm, as well as his family's Hotel Weissbrau and Brewery. The recipes came from Prince Luitpold of Bavaria, where the same beers are brewed at Kaltenberg Castle. Early on, they made friends with the owners of Bayern Brewery in Missoula, Montana. "One of the owners was a brewmaster and brewery technician and was very helpful in solving some issues we had and actually flew out to help us with the system. We ended up buying a lot of hops and yeast from them because they had the proper German yeast we needed. So Jorg was brewing up until about 2007, and I brewed from 2005 to 2007," Andy recounted.

Despite the German purity laws and Oklahoma's antiquated 3.2 beer laws, the brewery turned out three original beers that people raved about. "We're now called the best-hidden secret in Oklahoma," he told *Southwest*

The original brewhouse at Royal Bavaria watches over patrons behind a wall of glass. *Courtesy of Royal Bavaria.*

Brewing News. "People come through here all the time amazed that they can find such great beer in Moore, Oklahoma. We get calls from California asking how we make such great beer." The Kings Gold, a light lager, was based on a medium-bodied and unfiltered Munich helles beer. The King's Weizen, a traditional weissbier, was produced with a weissbier ale yeast that brought out notes of clove and banana. The dunkelweizen, or dark wheat beer, is brewed with roasted malts to impart a caramelized color and taste along with those found in the weissbier. Probably the most popular beer is the Oktoberfest, an amber-hued marzenbier with rich and toasty characters and mild hop bitterness. All of the beers went through a five-week lagering process to produce the smoothest beer possible. "If you let it ripen itself without disturbing the liquid at all," said Jorg, "you get the best results." Around 2008, Andy hired Garrick Ritzky to help brew as the restaurant was gaining more success. "We did a complete overhaul on the system," recalled Andy. "We used open fermentation until about 2009, and I wanted to move away from that because up until then we only had three beers and I wanted to expand to other varieties." While experimenting with the technique can be fun, Andy chose a more secure and consistent method to keep his customers happy and drink the same beer. However, when he and Garrick changed up the weizen beer from a lager yeast to an ale yeast, the flavor profile completely changed and a lot of customers did not like it. It went from his top-selling beer to barely selling at all. "Once we got our customers a little more educated and more of them branched out and tried a true Weizen beer imported into the States; people adapted and grew to like it a lot more," said Andy.

An authentic German restaurant wouldn't be complete without a beer garden. With seating for two hundred people, a dance floor and a stage, the beer garden made Royal Bavaria a desirable destination point in the spring and summer months. Every May, they would tap a ceremonial keg to open the beer garden to customers. After it was established, live music outside soon became a nuisance to local neighbors. Luckily, it was mediated among the city and local residents, and they were able to continue with the bands. "When I bought the restaurant in 2008, I had a completely different vision for the beer garden," said Andy. "I ripped out all the furniture and landscaped it, added a better stage with lighting, and started the music back up, but that's when we started running into problems and ended up being in a lawsuit that we luckily came out unscathed." The beer garden added tremendous value for his patrons, and he fought defiantly to keep it. Many amenities you see in German beer gardens, like a music stage and places for children to play and be entertained, were what brought guests back. Over the years, it served as a venue for birthday parties and weddings.

The same care is taken with the quality of food served alongside these lagered beers. "I keep close contact with colleagues in Germany," Gmeiner told the *Oklahoman* newspaper. "We change our menu consistently and update it as food changes in Germany." As for the ingredients themselves, all produce is organic, while the meat is free of chemicals. "If I don't want to eat it, I won't serve it," said Gmeiner. "You will only have a good end result if you start with a good product." One of the reasons they are successful to this day is the attention paid to customers' requests and catering to their needs. It's a simple philosophy that is backed up with more than thirty-five years in the restaurant industry. "Listen to the customer and make adjustments as long as we can stick to our values of pure German traditions in food and beer." That being said, you won't ever see burgers or chicken fingers on the kid's menu. "The day we put a hamburger on the menu to appease a certain customer base is the day I am no longer a part of the restaurant," said Andy poignantly. In his experience, people come out to Royal Bavaria for an experience and a traditional menu that can't often be found in Oklahoma. When the new alcohol reform laws took place in 2016, a lot of his customers requested Andy not change up his beers. "I would say almost 70 percent of our customers said don't make it stronger. The reason being, we are a fun place where you socialize; mainly because we don't have T.V. lots of people will stay 2 or 3 hours. We are between the 4.6% to 5.2% beers and received mixed feedback from people who liked it and some that know they have to be careful not to drink too much." Overall, it has given Andy a little freedom to brew his beers to style and brew in the more traditional manner that was intended like making a bock or double bock that would push 8 percent ABV. "The way I look at this industry, most breweries have people involved that are passionate about beer, and our goal is to educate more Oklahomans that there is other beer than Bud, Miller and Coors and shift the momentum to drink handcrafted brews," Andy stated.

Pete's Place (1995–Present)

In the quaint city of Krebs, about two hours south of Tulsa, lies the historic birthplace of Choc beer in a family restaurant called Pete's Place. As described earlier, Pete Prichard founded the restaurant after an unfortunate mining accident. He took up cooking for local miners and serving them homebrew. The beer lasted as a tradition up until around the mid-1980s. Joe Prichard, an Oklahoma State grad with a degree in hotel and restaurant management, was the third generation and took ownership of the restaurant after his father passed away in 1994. He struck up a conversation with co-worker and family friend Michael Lalli in the summer of 1994. "Wouldn't it be cool to bring back some of the old Choc brewing histories and have that at the restaurant?" he asked. Michael agreed and had been homebrewing with a neighbor of his at the time. Oklahoma lawmakers had recently passed the brewpub law, and the seed of the idea was planted. "I was in Colorado snowboarding and broke my ankle so I was homebound for a while, and Joe said this was a perfect opportunity to do some research, buy some equipment, and when I get back to work let's start brewing," recounted Michael.

How coincidental that two unfortunate leg injuries founded and rekindled the success of Choc Brewing. Being a beer geek, Michael had a good friendship with Bricktown's head brewer, Doug Moeller. "I called him up and asked if he'd help us try to figure out how to put this whole thing together, and sure enough he was all for it." A short time later, the seven-barrel Specific Mechanical brewhouse was up and running with two fermenters for the first batch of legal Choc beer, brewed on October 13, 1995. Michael developed an American amber, a peach ale and the Miner's Lite shortly after that were served alongside the family-style Italian cuisine. Coined as "Krebs hospitality," Pete's Place embodied a connected community with deep Italian heritage.

In an effort to spread the word, Michael proudly served them at local beer festivals like Mesta Festa, Tulsa Brewing's Brewfest and Bricktown's Oktoberfest to promote the new brand. At the Ethnic Festival in Krebs, for instance, nine kegs of Choc and thirty-one gallons of homemade root beer were floated. He quickly made friends with other brewmasters in the area and actually brewed his first beer at Bricktown. In the summer of 1997, an expansion was in the works for additional fermenters and cold storage for ingredients like hops and yeast. In 1996 alone, they brewed about five hundred barrels, which was a lot of work for two small fermenters at the time. Michael enjoyed experimenting with recipes, like one for a pumpkin spiced ale during the fall of 1997, when he had to lower his fermentation temperature to bring out more of the Briess malt character in his beer.

Pete's endured a big upgrade in the brewhouse and restaurant in what came to be known as Phase 98. Seating capacity rose from 350 to 525 with the addition of ten rooms and a small bar where customers could enjoy the local brew before the family-style meal. Michael's wish list was fulfilled, as he stated, "We will be installing an additional cold room for the grundies." Grundies were known as small UK-built pub cellar tanks that fit about 3.5 to 7 barrels for fermenting, conditioning or bright beer storage. Recipe changes were also added, as Michael substituted the Cascade hop, which was gaining popularity in the market, over the Liberty hop for his Choc beer; this added "a crispness and hops aroma, with no increase in bitterness." One of the painstaking jobs for Michael was personally filling every bomber bottle of Choc for distribution. A bottling line was added in 1999 to relieve him of those duties and help with a new venture in providing contract brewing services.

Choc was an iconic beer, as it became the first Oklahoma-made beer to be served at the Great State Fair of Oklahoma in 2003. Canning was in the works once the label was approved, marking the first time an Oklahoma beer was placed in an aluminum can. By now, Choc was selling so fast it was hard to keep up with demand, so they purchased new equipment in June 2004. Michael continued brewing with longtime friend Doug Moeller and created his first lager, an Oktoberfest, for the fall of 2004. In the spring of 2005, a new packaging area was added with more storage and new conditioning tanks, as well as an improved bottling line. Word spread fast of their ability to contract-brew and even led to brewing specialty beers for local eateries like the Double Deuce beer for Cattleman's Steakhouse in Oklahoma City and a beer for Louie's Restaurant and Deli. That summer, a second expansion saw the addition of several hundred square feet to a brewery, nearly doubling in size every batch of beer produced. A stronger version of Choc was eventually brewed to be packaged and sold in liquor stores.

THE ICE HOUSE & CHOCTAW AVENUE BREWING COMPANY (1998–2000)

Down in the historic city of McAlester was an icehouse built in 1897 near the KATY rail line that ran through Missouri, Kansas and Texas. McAlester and the surrounding area held large deposits of coal, as the mining industry was established in 1870. Ice plants were rather common near rail lines to stock refrigerated cars with ice for long trips. The Choctaw Ice & Cold Storage Company served until the early 1980s and was preserved as a historical landmark on the National Register of Historic Places in 1979. The dilapidated structure was put on the market in the early 1990s and eventually salvaged by local businesspersons Chris and Karin Clark. "Part of the building was erected in 1894," Chris told *Southwest Brewing News* reporter Matt Alcott. "An addition was added on to the former ice house around 1916. The building was set to be demolished and after 18 months of extensive remodeling, we can seat around 700 guests. We have a fully staffed kitchen that serves pizza, sandwiches, slow-roasted ribs, Mahi Mahi, Orange Roughy, and traditional pub fare." The project was spurred out of a deep respect for local history and the Clarks' love of music. In what was soon referred to as the "Ice House Project," demolition of the building revealed a solid interior structure and native rock wall. The former icehouse was redeveloped from a three-story building into a bar and music venue with amphitheater-style seating for concerts.

Curator of Krebs History Museum Steve DeFrange noted:

> *Stepped-down amphitheater seating was constructed comprising sixteen box seating cubicles that descend into the original basement. A sound stage approximately six feet high from the original basement level was erected, and a hardwood dance floor laid between the stage and the front lower box seats. A native rock floor was laid and a large horseshoe bar was constructed at the front end of the music venue room. A 30 by 20 foot opening was cut in the upper floor, in front of and above the stage to allow balcony seating for major concerts. The remainder of the 200 year old salvaged pine floor joists were finished to build usable countertops abound the box seats, freestanding tables, and bar tops.*

Originally, the top floor served as a recording studio, along with accommodations for visiting artists. Famous acts such as the Marshall Tucker Band, Edgar Winter, Molly Hatcher, the Nitty Gritty Dirt Band, .38 Special and Blue Öyster Cult performed at the venue at least once a month, with other live local music every weekend.

Steve DeFrange, a local homebrewer and close friend of Michael Lalli, started brewing out of his garage in 1984. "Steve is one of those guys in Krebs that knows everyone," said Lalli. "He figured out some modern techniques in brewing Choc that tastes more traditional and [is] easily replicated." According to Steve, he brewed out of tradition, as the early Italian immigrants had back in early statehood. An engineer employed at Spirit AeroSystems in McAlester, Steve had been brewing up Choc beer in his garage on an eight-barrel brewhouse system he had built himself out of a forty-nine-year-old steam kettle that he converted to natural gas and wrapped in copper. His fermenters were thirty-five-year-old modified milk

A Handcrafted History

Ice House sign. *Courtesy of Steve DeFrange.*

Ice House restaurant/music venue. *Courtesy of Steve DeFrange.*

storage tanks. Brewing to save a little money since the early 1970s, Steve decided that he wanted a brewery of his own. Several times he ventured up to Tulsa to Mecca Coffee Supply to purchase homebrewing materials and any literature he could find on brewing. "The Choc that was made here, it wasn't made very scientifically. It was a single fermentation and people made it as quick as they could on the chance they may get busted," said Steve. "A lot of my family and friends over the 12 years I brewed had been pushing me to open my own brewery, and I really didn't want to go through the trouble and the laws weren't set up yet to do so," recalled Steve. However, in 1996, he and his wife vacationed to Italy, and once he cleared his mind, he got serious and decided he'd open a brewpub in McAlester. Steve traveled to regional breweries in Arkansas and Texas and visited the new brewpubs in Oklahoma for research. Teamed up with his wife, sister-in-law and brother-in-law, they sought out a location where Steve could brew. The plan was for the two women to manage a small restaurant portion, and his brother-in-law would handle the paperwork and accounting. Unfortunately, his in-laws pulled out of the business venture, and Steve eventually found a piece of property to build his brewpub on. Coincidentally, they had looked at the Ice House as a potential location but decided that it needed too much restoration for their small endeavor.

In the middle of the new Ice House construction, Chris Clark thought it would be a great idea to have a brewhouse with locally made beers on tap. A mutual friend introduced the two of them, and after a meeting over some beers, they hashed out an agreement. After about a year and a half, the brewery was trucked over as the new brewhouse in the summer of 1998.

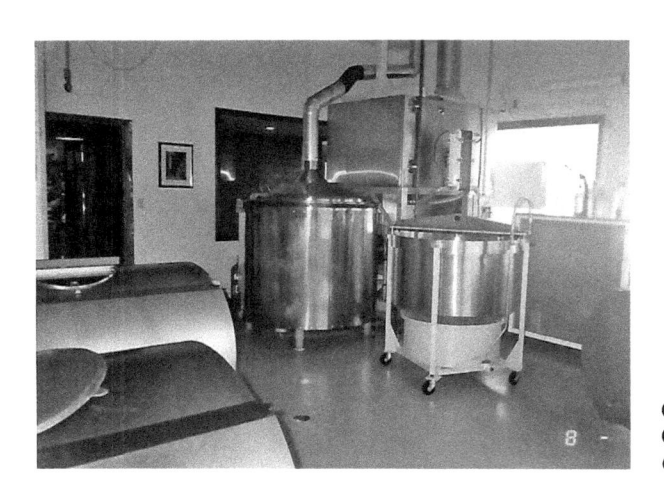

Choctaw Avenue Brewing Company's brewhouse. *Courtesy of Steve DeFrange.*

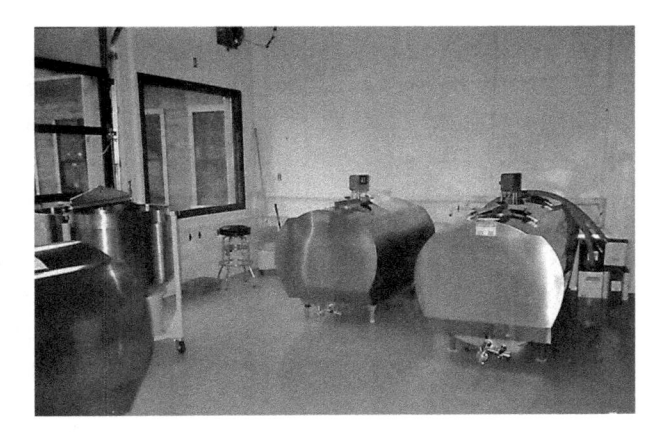

A Handcrafted History

Right: Choctaw Avenue Brewing Company's brewery. *Courtesy of Steve DeFrange.*

Below: Choctaw Avenue Brewing Company's sign. *Courtesy of Steve DeFrange.*

Steve created four unique beers for the bar. The Choctaw Draw was a light ale with rye malt, and the Choctaw Dark was like a porter or bock style that used sorghum to cut the bitterness of the dark malts and add a little sweetness. Two seasonal brews were an apple ale and an unnamed spiced ale brewed with cloves, ginger and orange peel. Steve was finally living out his dream, splitting time between his day job and brewing nights and weekends under the name Choctaw Avenue Brewing, based on the street where the Ice House was located.

It was unfortunately short-lived. One day in 1999, Steve and his wife went to pick up his birthday present. "His wife bought him a new motor scooter and as he drove it back from McAlester, Steve was run over by a Lincoln town car. He lost his right leg from the knee down and was decommissioned for a while. I ended up kegging beer off the bright tanks to keep the beer on tap for them," said Lalli. Eventually, Steve bounced back to brewing for about a year, after which the disability became too much to bear and he had lost his passion for brewing. "The place was still going well but I decided to shut it down and move the equipment back home and store it away," said Steve. The restaurant closed down not too long after, and the Clarks went back to the East Coast to their original business of building floating marinas. Steve continued to brew out of his home for the pure joy of it until he finally sold off the equipment in 2014. Currently, Steve can be found at the Krebs Heritage Museum, where he curates and preserves the Choc brewing history and runs the day-to-day operations.

Under Contract: T. Paul's Beer Company & Barleyfield Brewing

"Good Beer for Bad People." That was the slogan for the company of T. Paul Eagleton, University of Texas law graduate with a master's degree in tax law. "I was trying to find a business to open my whole life. In the early '90s, I was skiing in Crested Butte and went into a brewpub and drank some great beer. I got to thinking to myself, Tulsa doesn't have anything like this, and it seemed like a successful business. So, when I got back, I did some research and noticed that microbrewing was growing at 40 percent a year across the country," he said in an interview with the author. With an untapped market, he dedicated two years of his life learning the business and acquired a general manager position in Napa, California, just a short forty-five-minute drive from UC–Davis, where he studied biochemistry on nights and weekends and managed the brewery for about a year. His second year of "training" consisted of opening up a brewpub in Lake Tahoe by the name of Bluewater Brewing. He returned to Tulsa in October 1994 with a vision but needed some help in the sales department. Enter Rick Bahlinger, the former president of Budweiser distributing in Tulsa. They met through a mutual friend, and the rest is history. "We first came out with a 3.2 ABW or 4 percent ABV beer named T-Towne Red Ale." The brew was a Scotch ale with a malty flavor but not too bitter. "I'm a hop head and I always have been. I loved West Coast citrusy IPA, but I thought it would be a bridge too far for Tulsa going from light macro lagers to an IPA. I thought I should do a darker, maltier beer to show people the difference," recalled T. Paul. Right out the gate, there was an issue with educating the consumer, who at the time conflated 3.2 beer with bland beer and believed that the only quality beer was at the liquor store. As T. Paul reported to the author, "Guinness is a low ABV beer and it's a fine beer. Alcohol strength and the quality of the beer are unrelated things." They were pushing a higher-end product found in the liquor stores and were able to self-distribute since it was a 3.2 beer. His partner, Rick, would sell the beer to local accounts, and T. Paul would follow in a Bronco and deliver the beer. "Oklahoma law back then you had to have 4-inch letters with your license on any delivery vehicle, and everybody quickly got out of my way because they thought I was a cop."

With intentions of being an Oklahoma beer, they expanded their horizons and found accounts in neighboring states of Missouri and Kansas. "We tried to get into Arkansas and met with the wholesaler whose office was in a bank with a huge vault," said T. Paul. The long and short of it came down to go kick rocks basically. "Our product was in a bottle. The wholesaler said, 'Let me tell you something, boys. 80% of the beer drunk in Arkansas is out of a can that came out of a cooler in the woods. And that's not what you have.' I said no, we sure don't, and that was the end of that." They did attend some beer festivals in the Natural State and sold a lot of merchandise. Sales picked up as their beer was hitting shelves with partner Rick Bahlinger at the helm. At the time, there were only four or five major liquor stores in Tulsa, and this did not lead to many distribution opportunities. You could find their beer in Reasor's and Albertsons, two major grocery chains, as well as QuikTrip and Get 'n' Go convenience stores. As folks caught on to the new beer after a few months, they ran into an issue that plagued Oklahoma.

"Microbrewing was exploding all over the country. The people drinking our beer are adventurous drinkers; they're not brand loyal. They aren't bringing a six-pack of Bud home every Friday. They ask for what's new. So a few months later, here comes Samuel Adams and Pete's Wicked Ale and seasonal beers every month. We were a Tulsa company trying to be an Oklahoma beer. We called our beer T-Towne for Tulsa and even had a T-Towne Lager that was our lighter beer that we brought out, but I couldn't afford to build a brewery so we leased space in Dubuque Brewing and bottling up in Iowa," recalled T. Paul. Contract brewing was a fast way to bring products to market without investing hundreds of thousands in capital, which was the same method used by Samuel Adams. T. Paul would go up and brew about one hundred barrels at a time, then the company would bottle and package it and ship it back to Oklahoma. The T-Towne

Lager was a Vienna-style lager with an amber hue and was not too bitter for the style. At the time, it was a unique process because having a brewery that used two different kinds of yeast on its systems was a giant risk factor. "When people figured out that it was brewed and bottled in Dubuque, because we had to be transparent and put that on the label, many people that didn't know the whole story were offended. They thought we were pulling one over that maybe there's an OKC or Dallas Red Ale and it was just a marketing gimmick to pretend you're a local beer when you're not." Both partners did their best by putting flyers in the six-packs to try and educate consumers and ease their suspicions.

In an effort to help market themselves as a local brewer, they put together six beer festivals. They started with two Mardi Gras parties at the Castle of Muskogee, a large event venue in Muskogee, Oklahoma. Between the two partners, those weren't as successful as the Blues and Brews festivals held in the Brady Arts district of Tulsa. These were open to the public, where patrons paid for a cup to experience the beer festival portion. Instead of gating everything off and charging folks an entry fee, this plan seemed to entice more people to come out and buy merchandise and listen to free music. Since T. Paul was distributing through Coors, the large beer truck was also there selling beer to patrons. At the final festival, they made a nice profit, and the next day, Sunday, was supposed to put them well over the top. "I remember at our last Blues and Brews festivals there were bad storms coming in and possible tornadoes," recalled Rick. "All the local news stations were telling people don't go to the Blues festival, and we are just panicking and watching money invested in the event go down the drain." However, one of the hottest bands of the time, Indigenous, was rolling through town on tour, and thanks to T. Paul's relationship with KMOD, they got the band to stop and play for a crowd of nearly twelve thousand. Rick added, "They literally pulled their truck up to the back of our stage, unloaded, played our concert, loaded back up and went on to their next destination."

At the high point of their enterprise, Rick was hitting accounts weekly in Oklahoma City, and distribution was across the state. "We had boots on the ground working hard trying to get to $1/10^{th}$ of 1 percent market share; if we hit that we'd have still been in business," lamented Rick. Byron's in Oklahoma City brought T. Paul to its store to talk about beer and brewing while it held a sampling in a separate facility, since it was illegal to hold them at the liquor store. About this time, they met with a brewery named Pony Express from Olathe, Kansas, at a beer festival looking to get into

A Handcrafted History

Above: Paul Eagleton of T. Paul's Beer Company pours a beer at the Brews & Blues festival. *Photo by Emmanuel Lozano.*

Left: Barleyfield Brewing Company's Redding Premium Golden Ale bottle. *Courtesy of Jeff Swearengin.*

the market with its Tornado Ale. "They hired us to represent and market his beer in Oklahoma. We didn't have any of the licenses to actually carry them." Their best account in Tulsa was the airport because whenever anyone flew into town, they wanted to drink something local. Their second best was a place called the Snooty Fox, a gastropub-style restaurant and bar that mainly served British-style ales.

At the end of it all, they had good support but not enough diverse products to continue, and as both men were raising their young families, they needed a more stable work life. "We eventually sold to Coors, our distributor, in the end," recalled Rick. "Not that we had an amazing product and were driving out their competition necessarily, but they wanted our premium shelf space in the grocery and convenience stores." This was certainly the game being played for market share in the major retailers. "It wasn't that I was just a brewer, I had immersed myself in the education of craft brewing because I didn't know which way I was going to go with it. So I studied and tried to understand every piece of it and acquired some practical and technical knowledge and everything in between to make a clean, quality beer that Tulsans could call their own," T. Paul concluded.

Barleyfield Brewing Company

Charles (Charlie) and Michell Culbreath, owners and operators of Mecca Coffee Company, were avid beer and wine enthusiasts. For decades, Mecca was the aptly named place for homebrewing supplies for hobbyists and homebrewers in Tulsa. From equipment to extract kits and brewers yeast, Mecca supplied everyone from the novice to experts like the local brewpubs in 1994. Charles, along with partners Davis Redding and oil businessman Ty Thacker, started the Barleyfield Brewing Company, which brewed under a license at August Schell in New Ulm, Minnesota, and whose products were available in select markets in Oklahoma, Kansas, Missouri and Arkansas. Davis, who graduated from the Brewing Institute in London, was the brewmaster. The group went a different route than did T. Paul's and brewed a strong beer out of the gate at 5.3 percent ABV. This meant they had to go through a distributor to sell their beer. "It's as clean-tasting as a beer can possibly be," said Charlie to *Oklahoma Today* magazine.

As described in the magazine, the golden ale was brewed as a lager, aging it for thirty days with a fresh hop leaf and oak chip additions. "Beer needs to be aged," said Culbreath. "It smooths it out. It just makes it a

A Handcrafted History

Barleyfield Brewing Company's Redding Premium Golden Ale coaster depicts the history of the contract brewer. *Courtesy of Jeff Swearengin.*

better quality beer." Their philosophy was written out on promotional beer coasters that stated the same sentiments. "What sets Redding apart? Why is it at the top of the list when compared to other beers? It doesn't have a lite beer taste or a gimmicky flavored taste. It is a beer that people can identify with that wants a pure beer made in the Old World tradition. Beer is only as pure as the ingredients used and only the finest quality ingredients are used in Redding Premium Golden Ale." It continued, "Redding Premium Golden Ale was inspired by the classic ales of the Rhine Valley. It is microbrewed from a blend of wheat and two-row barley malts. Only the finest available German varieties of finishing hop flowers are used in the brewing process. A special German ale yeast adds a unique flavor and aroma. Redding Premium Golden Ale is cold conditioned with oak at temperatures near freezing for a smooth, clean taste….Enjoy!" The company started up not long after T. Paul's and only sold packaged bottles to liquor stores. It was a much smaller scale and only lasted about a year, folding in late 1996.

A CRAFT OF THEIR OWN, 2003–2015

Brewers tend to be equal parts romance and work ethic: Show up early, run into problems throughout the day, cancel dinners with girlfriends, head home under a night sky—only to wake up and do it again the next day. The rewards are sparsely peppered throughout the years, and they usually don't relate to money or living a healthy lifestyle. It's the kind of work that leaves your back sore and your wallet thin. But there are moments of unexplainable gratification, if you're paying close attention.
—*Jake Miller, Heirloom Rustic Ales*

HUEBERT BREWING COMPANY (2003–2014)

At the time of this writing, craft brewing in Oklahoma has come a long way since microbreweries were first allowed to operate in 2003. Laws prior to that time restricted anyone from opening a production brewery to brew strong beer for distribution. There had been attempts in 2000 to sway conservatives in the capitol to realize the benefits of the industry. Despite the generous incentive of tax revenue gains, these efforts were unanimously shot down. A frustrated college kid got the brewing itch when he didn't feel like sneaking around or paying someone to buy him beer. This was before homebrewing had become legal in the state, when supplies were cobbled together like barley from a local feed store. He eventually joined a few brew heads while researching brewing at the school library and formed the High Plains Draughters club. Near the end of his college days, he met Shaneen,

A Handcrafted History

his future wife, and flat out told her, "My aspiration is to own a brewery. If you have a problem with that, you don't want to be with me." Harsh words that would turn most away, but Shaneen saw the passion and drive and was immediately all in. Eventually, he found work as a technician at a food production plant.

By 1998, Rick Huebert and his wife had invested in brewing equipment for more than ten years, storing it at a farm in central Oklahoma until he found a facility to house it. However, he couldn't legally brew strong beer for distribution. So, with help from state senator Kathleen Wilcoxson and a lobbyist from the Oklahoma Malt Beverage Association (OMBA), they authored a bill that lowered or nearly eliminated the license fee for a brewer and allowed breweries to sell to liquor distributors and the public. Senate Bill 353 also eliminated employees from having to be licensed. "For small breweries, this law provides tax incentives," said Oliver Delany, then president of the OMBA. "What he ended up with is permissive legislation. It's very pro-business." Huebert reported to the *Oklahoman*, "I had to learn my way through the system, both at the state and federal levels."

In 2003, the Hueberts officially opened their brewery at 421 Southwest Twenty-Sixth in the Capitol Hill area of Oklahoma City. After securing a 6,500-square-foot facility that could house his collection of used equipment, Rick handcrafted his first microbrewed craft beer for distribution. Old Tyme Lager was an amber-hued lager with a 6.2 percent ABV and was reminiscent of an English beer. A 3.2 version was brewed for people to drink on-premise. Everything was bottled on his innovative bottling line that used a hairdryer to help remove runoff and allow the labels to stick better. In the summer of 2004, Rick was picked up by two distributors, which paved the way for him to market his beers to restaurants and liquor stores in Oklahoma City. After tinkering in the malt-flavored beverage market through a contract job, Rick developed Rock Hard Root Beer, an alcoholic root beer that certainly was ahead of its time before the trendy Not Your Father's Root Beer hit the markets. His son Aaron wanted his own drink, so Rick took out the fermenting process and made Round Barn Root Beer. It soon became an instant hit at the new Pops soda-themed restaurant and convenience store. He later developed a beer, aptly named Hops, exclusively for the tourist attraction that catered to Route 66 fans.

There were many learning curves, like when Rick changed bottle suppliers due to cost increases in 2009. "As we ran them through the bottling line, we ended up with a bunch of crushed bottles," reported Rick to the *Southwest Brewing News*. A few modifications later, he managed to refit the new bottle size to his line. "Our bottling process is way more labor-intensive than the other guys', but it ensures a more stable product on the shelves." Rick eventually upgraded in 2010 to a Crown Filler bottling system, cutting fill time from around thirteen hours down to about three. Output increased almost tenfold from seven hundred bottles an hour to nearly ten thousand. In the fall of 2011, Rick added three new thirty-two-barrel fermenting tanks; he and Chris Sanders, his head brewer, developed four new beers to fill them. Wild Pony Wheat, Tucker Pale Ale, Rasenmaher (a German-style kolsch) and Deep Deuce Porter were bottled and sold in six-packs for distribution. Right around this time, Chris left to join the OK City Brewing Co-Op with his own endeavor to open a brewery.

Huebert didn't take it lightly that he was brewing a very niche product in a state that was overrun with mass-produced yellow fizzy water. Rick made national headlines with his Nobama Brew, a red ale that took a jab at Barack Obama in 2012 during his campaign. "The phones keep ringing off the hook and my email keeps locking up. I can't make the beer fast enough for the demand," recounted Rick. Initially, Rick wanted to make this beer available throughout the country, but the TTB denied it and said it was only for sale in Oklahoma. Along with his Rock Hard series, Rick developed several concoctions like the Strawberry Daiquiri, which was not carbonated and paid homage to the Cuban Fresca daiquiri. These were alcohol-based drinks that were bagged and sold to accounts like the Texas Rangers and Oklahoma City Thunder.

Rick had quite a few irons in the fire at this point and had formed a good relationship with the folks at Bricktown Brewery. "As we were growing, we needed a larger space to help brew our beers, so we rented space in Rick's brewery to accommodate that," said Charles Stout, area manager for Bricktown. "We were there doing the brewing, trucking the grain over and mashing in and using his equipment and fermenters, kegging it and shipping it out to all of our restaurants. We did this from 2015 up to 2019, and during that time, we added more restaurants…at one point he came to us and said it was probably time for him to move on. He had gotten out of the beer end of the business and focused primarily on the hard-soft drinks for a while. I think he was just finished and wanted to get out. We came to an agreement where he sold us the property and equipment and brewed out of both facilities for a few years." Within the agreement, the property was given back to Rick, as Bricktown has since moved on to contract-brew in Krebs. The property remains dormant, possibly waiting for the next up-and-coming brewer.

A Handcrafted History

Krebs Brewing Company (2004–Present)

Originally known as the Choc Brewing Company, the brewery changed its name to Krebs Brewing Company in November 2004 and saw the beginning of a larger-scale expansion with a planned release of six year-round beers, spanning six chapters of Pete Prichard's life in Oklahoma. Waving Wheat, a Belgian-style witbier, was a hazy wheat beer with notes of citrus and spicy clove character paired perfectly with the summer heat. Miner Mishap emulated a schwarzbier that was formulated by local award-winning homebrewer Shawn Scott. Basement Batch, a well-balanced pale ale, was brewed with Cascade and Centennial hops with pine aromas and biscuit sweet malts. 1919, an American-style wheat ale with fruity lemon scents and bready malts, paid homage to the original Choc. Pietro Piegari, an amber ale, was brewed with caramel sweetness and a slight hop bitter finish. The final chapter, the Last Laugh, was an American white ale brewed with coriander seeds, giving it a fruity yet spicy flavor.

Accolades soon followed after Krebs's 1919 beer won a medal in the GABF in Colorado. Over the next few years, Michael would go on to develop more award-winning beers. He experimented with a farmhouse-style ale found in the northern region of France known as a *biere de garde*. It won consecutive medals at the North American Beer Awards in 2007 and 2008. Then, in the summer of 2009, Choc took home a silver medal in the Belgian Wit category for its Waving Wheat. His Signature Belgian-Style Dubbel won a gold medal in the Belgian-Style Abbey Ale category at the GABF, beating out fifty-seven other beers in 2009. "We knew going into the festival that we had submitted a great beer, but we also knew it would be one of the most fiercely entered categories," Zach Prichard, owner of Choc Beer Company, told the *Tulsa World*. The initial brew did not go as intended, as when Michael went to check on the Belgian yeast starter, he said it smelled of nail polish, which is a bad sign. Naturally, he drove up to the nearest homebrew supplier, High Gravity in Tulsa, and purchased all of its Trappist yeast strains. "I'm not going to lie to you," Lalli told Mike Averill of the *Tulsa World*. "It was pretty fun walking across the stage with the guy who started the Brewer's Association handing out the medals. That's pretty cool." Due to that success, Choc released a new set of Brewmaster Series beers that started with a Belgian-style quad, a *biere de garde* and a super saison in January 2010. Its 1919 beer took a silver medal in the American-Style Wheat Beer category at the Brewers Association World Beer Cup in 2012.

TABLE. KREBS BREWING COMPANY AWARDS, 2000–2011

2011	Signature Biere de Garde—Gold, North American Beer Awards Signature Smoked Porter—Silver, North American Beer Awards
2010	Signature Dubbel—Gold, North American Beer Awards Signature Belgian Quad—Silver, North American Beer Awards Waving Wheat—Bronze, North American Beer Awards Signature Belgian Quad—Bronze, World Beer Cup Miner Mishap—Bronze, European Beer Star
2009	Signature Dubbel—Gold, Great American Beer Festival Waving Wheat—Silver, North American Beer Awards
2008	Signature Biere de Garde—Bronze, North American Beer Awards
2007	Signature Saison—Silver, North American Beer Awards Signature Biere de Garde—Bronze, North American Beer Awards
2000	1919—Bronze, Great American Beer Festival

One reason Choc won so many awards could be attributed to paying attention to finer details and not putting its own spin on a classic style. In 2012, it revived a unique beer style brewed with wheat malt smoked over oak known as the Polish-style grätzer. Documented by Nick Trougakos for the *Oklahoman*, the award-winning beer was formulated under serendipitous circumstances with the help of local homebrewer William Scott. Scotty, as he was known, was intrigued by the beer and started tracking down the unique ingredients like a treasure hunter, looking for a style that had not been commercially brewed since 1994. The smoked wheat came about haphazardly, as Michael Lalli just called up his friends at Weyermann maltsters in Germany. "As it happened, they were having a meeting about new product lines and things like that," Scott said. "They replied right away, saying yeah, that's a great idea. It'll be on its way." After much research on Polish homebrew forums, Scotty was put in touch with a man in Warsaw who had some original strains of the yeast. It just so happened that he was about to take his wife on vacation in the next few weeks. Another stroke of luck involved the similar water profile found in Krebs; after a few mineral

Top: New State Beer label. *From beercoast.com.*

Middle: OK'a Special Brew beer label from Oklahoma Ice & Brewing Company. *From beercoast.com.*

Bottom: Ranger beer label from Ahrens Brewing Company. *From taverntrove.com.*

Above: "Dipping Beer out of the Streets of Oklahoma City after State-wide Prohibition Nov. 16th 1907; 28,000 barrels dumped in gutter by Revenue Officers." *Courtesy of Western History Collections, University of Oklahoma Libraries.*

Left: Bricktown Brewery's brewhouse installation. *From the* Oklahoman.

Above: Mustang Brewing Company brewmaster Gary Shellman looking at fermentation vessels sitting beneath the collapsed roof at the OKCity Brewing Cooperative building in Oklahoma City, June 10, 2013. The building was damaged in the May 31 storm. *Photo by Paul B. Southerland, from the Oklahoman.*

Right: Joe Prichard with his grandfather's crock, which was used to brew beer back in the 1920s at Pete's Place in Krebs, Oklahoma. *Photo by Bill Swindell.*

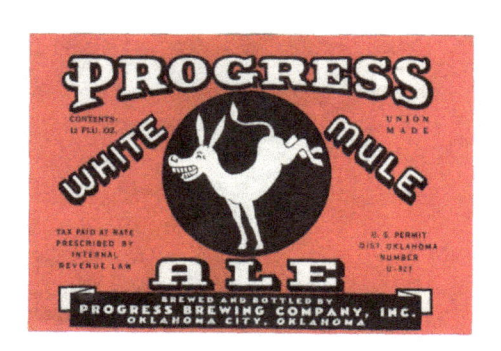

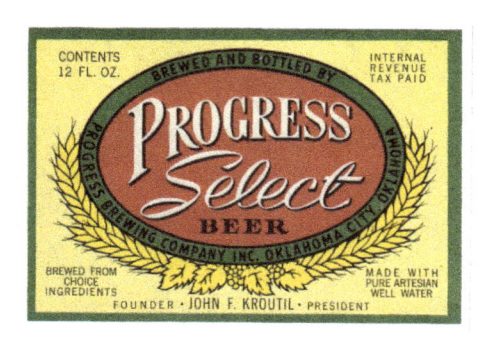

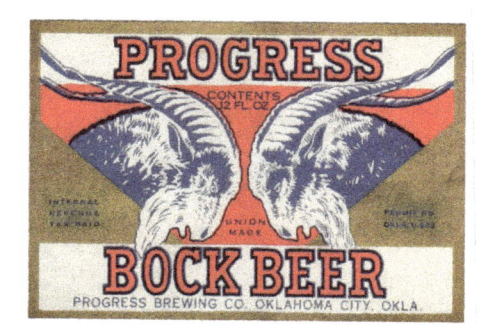

Top: Progress White Mule Ale label. *From beercoast.com.*

Middle: Progress Select Beer label. *From taverntrove.com.*

Bottom: Progress Bock Beer label. *From taverntrove.com.*

Anthem Brewing Company brewmaster Matt Anthony at his Oklahoma City headquarters, July 29, 2014. *Photo by David McDaniel, from the* Oklahoman.

Blaine Stansel readies the original taproom for customers in 2013 after the sampling bill passed. *Courtesy of Roughtail Brewing Company.*

From left to right: Taylor, Zac and Isaac Hanson in their office to promote Hop Jam on March 10, 2016. *Photo by Tom Gilbert/*Tulsa World.

Choc six-pack sampler in the studio on April, 2, 2009. *Photo by Tom Gilbert/*Tulsa World.

Top: Gold Seal Extra Dry Premium Beer label from Southwestern Brewing Corporation. *From taverntrove.com.*

Middle: Old King Beer factory scene, framed lithograph. *Courtesy of Dan Morean at breweriana.com.*

Bottom: OK Special Brew from Oklahoma Ice & Brewing Company. *From beercoast.com.*

Belle Isle's kitchen and brick oven. *Photo by the author.*

Tulsa Brewing Company head brewer Mike Groshong is living out his dream. *Courtesy of Jeff Swearengin.*

Tulsa Brewing Company's "On Tap Today" tap list, with brewery in the background. *Courtesy of Jeff Swearengin.*

Some of the beers that have been produced by Chase and Colin Healey at Prairie Artisan Ales brewery on October 3, 2013. *Photo by Tom Gilbert/Tulsa World.*

Top: Jayhawk Pilsener Beer label. *From beercoast.com.*

Middle: Golden Vienna Style Beer label from Southwestern Brewing Corporation. *From beercoast.com.*

Bottom: Old King Bock Beer label from Southwestern Brewing Corporation. *From beercoast.com.*

T. Paul's Beer Company six-packs of T-Towne Lager and T-Towne Red. *Courtesy of Rick Bahlinger.*

T. Paul's Beer Company owners, Sales and Marketing Director Rick Bahlinger (*left*) and brewer T. Paul Eagleton pose for a photo and keg of their brew. *Courtesy of Rick Bahlinger.*

Wooden beer crate of Old King Beer from Southwestern Brewing Corporation. *Courtesy of Sean Ball.*

Chase Healey, head brewer at COOP Ale Works, inspects the 217-gallon brewery tanks as the operation prepares to start distribution. *From the* Oklahoman.

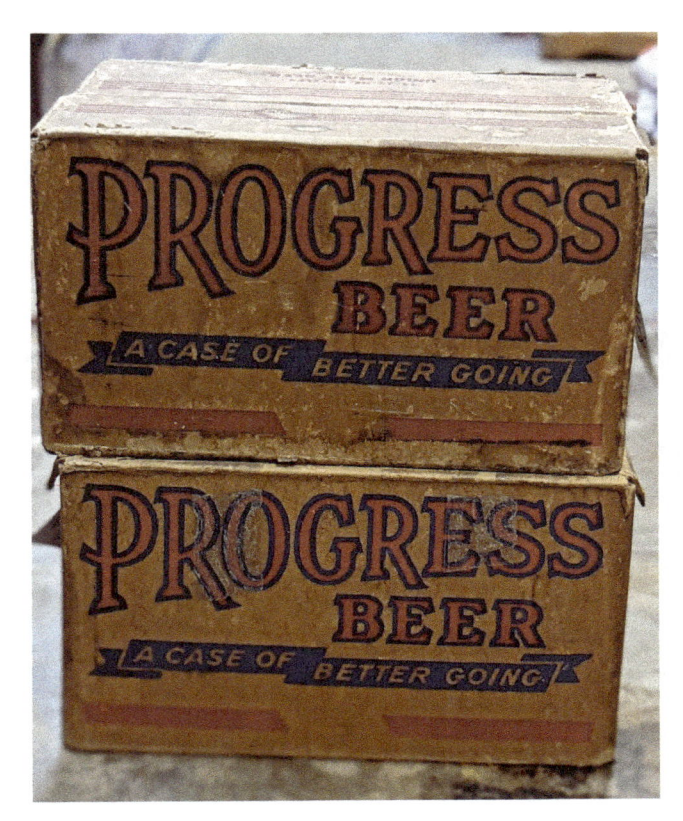

Progress Beer cases.
Photo by the author.

Progress Select's aluminum cone can. *Photo by the author.*

"Old King The Quality Beer from Southwestern Brewing Corporation." *Courtesy of taverntrove.com.*

Elk Valley's flagship beers. *Photo by Tom Gilbert.*

Right: Brewery owner Joe Prichard (*left*) and brewer Michael Lalli inside the Choc Beer brewery in Krebs, Oklahoma, on June 27, 2007. Choc Beer unveiled its new Basement Batch Pale Ale for the Fourth of July. *Photo by Tom Gilbert.*

Below: Front of Pete's Place restaurant at the Choc Brewery in Krebs, Oklahoma, on October 25, 2013. *Photo by Tom Gilbert.*

Ranger Beer tin sign from Ahrens Brewing Company. *Trey Rowe collection.*

The brew crew of Marshall Brewing Company celebrates its tenth anniversary. *Courtesy of Marshall Brewing Company.*

A Handcrafted History

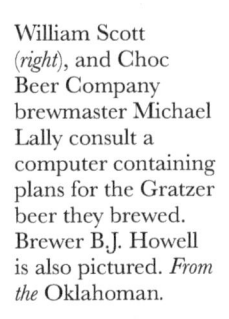

William Scott (*right*), and Choc Beer Company brewmaster Michael Lally consult a computer containing plans for the Gratzer beer they brewed. Brewer B.J. Howell is also pictured. *From the* Oklahoman.

alterations, they were able to match that as well. Finding the original hop strain, known as Nowotomyski, would not be possible, but Scotty substituted a Polish Lubliner hop that shared a common ancestry. Without Scott's countless hours perusing old brewing texts and documents, they might not have found the brewing schedule to actually make the beer. "You can kind of get bogged down in your normal production routine," Prichard said. "So it's really important to try to create new beers, or try to revive beers, or just do different things that are a challenge for us technically—so we stay fresh and stay really interested in the process."

Krebs has distributed beer to every continent except Africa and Antarctica, along with forty states here at home. "Opening in new geographic markets is exciting and necessary," Prichard said. "As our brewery has developed we have shifted toward even more experimental and progressive styles.…There are many beer fans who enjoy these beers; at the same time, there are not a lot in any one given market. To get our beer to these drinkers, we must be in many markets." This fortuitous premonition came true when a gypsy brewer by the name Chase Healey came around looking for a space to try out a new project known as Prairie Artisan Ales.

Marshall Brewing Company (2008–Present)

A fine beer may be judged with only one sip, but it's better to be thoroughly sure.
—*Czech proverb*

Close to the summer of 2004, an unprecedented establishment was opened the likes of which downtown Tulsa had never seen before. The area was a desert with little to no nightlife activities or hubs to frequent for a night out on the town. That changed when Elliot Nelson opened McNellie's Pub at First and Elgin. Harkening back to Irish-style pubs, it had elaborate wood bar tops, a full kitchen, two floors and sixty taps of microbrewed and imported beers. Around this time, Eric Marshall had just finished up his last final at Tulsa University, where he studied international business in German. He mentioned to Elliot his plans for a local brewery after a few years of apprenticeship. Eric regaled his origin story to a local podcast:

> *I lived in Germany for around 7 months and studied abroad with a family and just really loved the experience and also had the opportunity to drink a lot of fresh local beer and really dug the whole cultural aspect of it. When I got back I didn't have that same opportunity to drink good, fresh, local beer and at the time my brother Adam was home brewing a lot. We saw a real opportunity and began our research into a microbrewery.*

After he discussed his vision with some local church friends, they set up a meeting with their son's best friend, who just happened to be a German brewmaster from Munich. Stefan had helped as a consultant for the Royal Bavaria brewpub in Moore. As if the stars had aligned, Eric received a call the very next day, and once he graduated, he stepped into the next chapter of his life. Stefan gave him some options about going into brewing. "The four-year brewing degree from Weihenstephan, which is the oldest operating brewery, was quite prestigious, but I just finished a four-year degree. Or there was a program through the Doemens Academy in Munich, a private brewing academy, and they do a twin campus deal with Siebel Institute in Chicago which is called the World Brewing Academy and then you do some hands-on practical stuff in Germany." He mentioned, "We can get you into that and once you are done I have a bunch of contacts for apprenticing." Just like that, he had a plan and apprenticed in seven different places around Germany with a lot of odd jobs and consulting. Eric eventually ended up in Philadelphia at Victory Brewing.

Meanwhile, back in Tulsa, Adam and his dad were doing their due diligence about bringing Eric's newfound talents to Tulsa. The two brothers were longtime fans of *SCTV* comedy duo the McKenzie brothers, played by Rick Moranis and Dave Thomas, and loved the movie *Strange Brew*. So they had this passion and started scaling up their homebrew system from five to fifteen barrels. At the time, their dad was thinking of converting a spare room into a study, but as the boys kept brewing, he decided to create a Scottish pub instead. "So we got dad to finance the equipment, and we started to build the homebrew system that eventually became the pilot system for our brewery," reminisced Adam. While Eric was learning the trade at Victory in 2005, Adam had seen more places like Huebert and Choc making and selling craft beer. "So we start popping off e-mails back and forth trying to formulate a business plan, and I remember saying I think we can do this," Adam recalled.

"I always knew sooner or later I'd come back to Tulsa," Eric told the *Tulsa World*. "I love Tulsa. This is my home. This is where my family is and this is where I want to make my beer." For a city that hadn't seen a production brewery since the 1930s, the regulations were not well structured for an emerging industry. As they had an operating brewery, the city required them to be in a medium industrial zone. Finding capital was easy, but finding a facility proved one of the hardest steps. "We went through five contracts on five different buildings, with one owner not wanting to sell their building, people being unreasonable, and people just outright lying about the condition of their building," he told the *Journal Record*. Eric persevered and purchased a brew system secondhand from a brewery in Japan with

Eric Marshall digs up trenches for the brew floor. *Courtesy of Marshall Brewing Company.*

OKLAHOMA BEER

Above: Eric Marshall supervises as his brewhouse is being unloaded. *Courtesy of Marshall Brewing Company.*

Opposite: Marshall Brewing Company's brewhouse floor. *Courtesy of Marshall Brewing Company.*

stainless fermenters and copper mash tuns similar to what you would see in Germany. After months of installation and digging trenches for pipes in the 7,300-square-foot building, Eric was ready to brew.

Marshall Brewing Company fired up its kettles in the spring of 2008 and released its flagship beers Sundown Wheat, Atlas IPA and McNellie's Pub Ale in early summer of 2008. Sundown was brewed as a mix between Belgian-inspired and American wheat beers. Atlas IPA satiated the hop heads with a big malt backbone and intense hop character, measuring close to 7.5 percent ABV. Finally, McNellie's Pub Ale was brewed in honor of the local pub as a smooth and sessionable English bitter. Kegs for local accounts started the journey, and they brewed about five hundred barrels of beer that year. "To run a business you have to be able to sell your product and appeal to your local beer drinkers," Eric told the *Southwest Brewing News*. Wheat beers were certainly a transition beer and appealed to many light beer drinkers. Boulevard Wheat was prominent as a regional beer to many Oklahomans before the local movement took off. Naturally, Eric's time spent in Germany led him to brew a hefeweizen-style ale that slaked

A Handcrafted History

the thirst on many hot summer days. Marshall filled his flagship beers just in time for the holiday season, released in 750ml waxed bombers that debuted in liquor stores. The waxed tops were temporary, as the brewery would offer six-packs of twelve-ounce bottles in early 2009. "Oklahoma is a fun market because a lot of people are transitioning to drink craft beer," reported Eric to *Tulsa World*. The timing was well planned, as craft beer sales rose more than 10 percent in 2009 according to the Brewers Association. It was evident that Tulsa embraced Marshall's beer, available in 180 bars and restaurants and more than 200 retail stores in just a year and a half of opening. Sundown and Atlas were so popular that six-packs weren't available until December 2010.

"We were just selling too many of those beers on draft to have any leftover to bottle and to assure that we could keep the pipeline full," said Wes Alexander, director of sales and marketing. Wes, a family friend, offered up his help to Eric when the brewery concept was announced. While many accounts were asking for the product, it was helpful to have Wes on board to manage the madness and grow a nouveau business in Oklahoma. Nothing like this had been attempted in Tulsa since Ahrens Brewing Company shut down in 1940. Now that tastes had changed and the laws allowed for the distribution of full-strength beer, Marshall could brew a beer for Tulsans to enjoy and call their own. "The goal is to be part of the culture," Eric said. "To become 'local lore,' as they say."

Marshall released three original beers in twenty-two-ounce bombers and waxed tops. *Courtesy of Marshall Brewing Company.*

Eric's vision was to have four core beers and up to four seasonal beers that would be released around ten weeks and resonate with the seasons of Oklahoma. Old Pavilion Pilsner, a light German lager, rounded out the core offerings. Their first seasonal, Big Jamoke Porter, was named for the B-25 bomber Eric's grandfather flew in World War II. Appropriately, it was released in 22-ounce bomber bottles and boasted a blend of five malts with aromas of toffee and roasted coffee. In the fall of 2009, a malty Oktoberfest lager paid tribute to his time brewing in Germany. "Our first Oktoberfest was available only in kegs, and we made three batches," said Marshall. "This year [2010] we also bottled it, made 12 batches, and as it turned out, we could have sold a lot more." In 2011, the lager was available at Tulsa Oktoberfest and marked the first local craft beer offered alongside Krebs at the festival. To usher in the spring season, Marshall created a hop-forward American red ale, Revival Red, that featured six malts and citrus flavors from Chinook and Cascade hops. The fourth and final seasonal beer was Arrowhead Pale Ale, brewed with a new Citra hop, debuted on June 29, 2011, at Leon's in Broken Arrow. Citra hops were all the rage, and the first run only lasted forty-five days as demand for the new hop grew. In the fall of 2010, Eric unleashed the El CuCuy, which translates to Boogieman. Debuting at the Tulsa Press Club First Draft beer festival, the India black ale or Cascadian dark ale was dry hopped and blended with roasted malts and clocked in at 8.6 percent ABV.

With steady growth, an expansion was inevitable. Eric leased the six-thousand-square-foot building next door for warehouse space and doubled their cold tank storage in the summer of 2010. More storage meant more beer and the potential to expand regionally to states like Kansas. As of 2012, the company has seen 60 percent growth compared to 2010 after the expansion to draft and bottles in the Kansas market. Eric always had the mindset early on of being a small regional brewery. Other markets included neighboring states like Arkansas and Missouri. "I like the smaller regional approach, because we have a lot more control of our product," Eric told *Tulsa World*. By the spring of 2012, they had gone through three tank expansions and had hired a full-time brewer to keep up with demand. Marshall expanded organically through careful growth and not relying on investors or loans that could potentially hinder its output. With strategic marketing, Marshall hosted beer dinners with local restaurants, attended regional beer festivals and tirelessly put itself in front of the consumer. Marshall donated its spent grain to local Beach Family Farm in Bristow, which promoted community outreach and saved the farm almost 25 percent of grain feed costs. Its marketing was pure and consistent by continuously educating the consumer about the quality products it made in an industry that, when it started, only had about 5 to 6 percent of the market share of beer sold by volume.

Beer Sampling Bill

As they had a small distribution brewery, there were many times Eric was asked by fans if they could come and sample a beer in the taproom. Eric would sigh and confess that the alcohol laws didn't permit Oklahoma breweries to allow free samples. When the Alcohol Beverage Laws Enforcement commission conducted the brewery's inspection prior to opening, he put down the idea but passed along some names of state representatives who might be interested in making it a reality. Fast-forward to 2012 and House Bill 2477, authored by Seneca Scott of Tulsa, which sought to allow patrons ten ounces of free beer per visitor per day. Unfortunately, it was killed in March 2012 without being given a floor vote by the House of Representatives. "Right now, the law technically does not allow me to sample my own beer, and this is ridiculous," Eric Marshall said in a news release. "We are proud of what we've built in Tulsa, and when we have visitors to our brewery, we would like to extend a limited amount of hospitality with a very small sample of our product." Aimed at being a pro-business and pro-tourism bill for Oklahoma, it was no surprise there were legislators who refused to push a pro-alcohol bill through on their watch. While it had bipartisan support, they were left scratching their heads and decided to regroup and present it again in 2013.

Eric's brother and co-owner, Adam Marshall, was pivotal in writing the new bill. With help from Representative Glen Mulready of Tulsa, a new sampling bill was aimed to amend Section 521 of Title 37 to permit licensed brewers to provide visitors no more than twelve ounces of free samples per person per day. Ultimately, this bill would help even the playing field with local wineries, which could already serve samples to consumers. "The opportunity to explain the business and culture of craft beer and brewing to the public while offering small limited samples will help our industry grow, offer more jobs, pay more taxes, and create a culture of craft beer tourism similar to most other states like Colorado," said Eric to the *Oklahoman*. A three-year process showed the brothers that in order for the system to change, they had to get involved. Labeled at times as a pioneer for small businesses and breweries to come, Marshall Brewing paved a path for alcohol reform in Oklahoma. "We feel this bill will help Oklahoma's breweries grow craft culture through education and advocacy to all of Oklahoma, as well as develop a base for tourism in the region," said Wes Alexander. The bill was signed on April 22 and went into full effect on November 1, 2013, when Representative Glen Mulready tapped a cask-conditioned Topeca Coffee Big Jamoke Porter in Marshall's taproom. Along with the free samples, tours of the brewing facility educated the consumer on the process of making beer and created a more informed consumer.

Marshall continued to tinker with more robust beers when it aged a Russian imperial stout, Black Dolphin, aged in Heaven Hill barrels to lend flavors of vanilla and roast from the used charred oak bourbon barrels. Named for Russia's most intense maximum-security prison, the beer was released in waxed bomber bottles in January 2014. Later that spring, This Machine IPA, a Belgian-style IPA, was brewed "featuring the complexity created during fermentation using a Belgian yeast strain, and the light citrus aroma and flavor of the Nelson Sauvin hop," per the Marshall website. It then served as the base for Bound for Glory, which had been added to whiskey barrels previously containing Black Dolphin Stout, aged for a period of six to eight months. While Marshall celebrated more than five years of brewing with another barrel-aged beer in 2013 and with the success of the tasting law bringing in new clientele, it excelled by making low-point beers to sell on-premise. An idea that had generated among several Oklahoma breweries to offer a 3.2 percent ABW beer while guests visited the taproom gained traction and led to a new era for the Oklahoma craft beer industry. Marshall brewed up a bitter Mosaic Pale Ale for sale in pints and growlers to enjoy off-premise. "We are hopeful that Tulsans on Friday run by the grocery store, run by the bakery and run by the brewery and pick up a fresh growler of the Mosaic Pale Ale and take it home for the kitchen table," said Wes Alexander. Breweries were only allowed to fill their own growlers, and Marshall instituted an exchange program to ensure that people had clean growlers.

In 2014, Eric teamed up with friend and local restaurateur Elliot Nelson to create a sports bar brewpub in downtown Tulsa. "Elliot found the spot and had the concept and all of that. My role is to handle the brewery side of things," reported Eric to the *Tulsa World*. The seven- to ten-barrel brewhouse would make four to six house beers that were developed by Eric, and it brewed to a 3.2 ABW strength to comply with the brewpub laws. With a sports bar setting, it was a natural fit across the street from the minor-league Tulsa Drillers baseball stadium, where fans could gather for a local beer after a game. "We've had a lot of requests to put in a good sports bar downtown," Elliot told *Tulsa World*; at the time, they had already opened six successful restaurants in downtown Tulsa. Eric lent his creativity and brewing prowess to develop some low-point beers to be enjoyed with unique wood-fired pizzas and bar food. Eventually, Austin McIlroy would take over brewing duties before opening his own brewery in Tulsa.

Every year, there is a day called One Voice Day, where the public can visit the capitol in Oklahoma City and talk openly with legislators about issues concerning them. The Marshall brothers had done this for several years and successfully championed the tasting laws in 2013. After that, there was a sort of moral and political swing from conservatives that issues like alcohol laws didn't have to take up so much capital. The Marshalls voiced their concerns as a small business to shed light on the gains the state would make in tax revenue and increase tourism. As Adam Marshall said to the *Madness Media* podcast, "If you're not at the table, then you're on the menu." As proponents for spreading good beer culture in Oklahoma, Eric and Adam found themselves at the precipice of a new era concerning alcohol reform in February 2015.

COOP Ale Works (2009–Present)

Around 2006, two creatives found themselves looking at a meager cooler full of uninspiring beer folks brought to a "Beer and Bull" session hosted by the Central Chapter of the American Institute of Architects. "We were looking at the beer in there," J.D. Merryweather recalled, "and we talked about how sad it was that none of it was local. We saw that this could be a great niche." His colleague Mark Siebold concurred, which led to a three-year journey of epic research across regional and national breweries to learn how they operated and what beer styles would prove financially stable in the Oklahoma market. Daniel Mercer joined the enterprise as the third partner and oversaw the finances of the brewery along with four investor groups. A brewmaster was needed to develop these local beers, and the stars aligned perfectly when they met Chase Healey, an avid homebrewer who was still finishing up his college courses at Oklahoma University. "I was lucky enough to have this crazy timing, being in our backwards state and getting into the beer industry right out of college. Heck, I graduated while I was working there," Healey told *Tulsa World*. Like many other brewers, he got the brew bug early on in college with a standard beer kit and progressed to all-grain brewing.

On July 15, 2008, the COOP brand was born. The name derived from cooper, a barrel-maker, hence the anvil depicted on the logo. Many have thought it meant co-op, although they'd technically be correct, as it was a kind of collective of creatives who all shared an art background and came together to produce local beer for Oklahoma. "We develop our beers as a team; Chase brews a test-batch. Oftentimes we serve it up and we surprise everyone," Merryweather told *Southwest Brewing News*. Early in the development stages, everyone kept their day jobs and traveled to different parts of the country, keeping an eye out for popular local beers and finding the right style to fit their new brewery. A more formal trip to Denver consisted of four days of research at thirteen different breweries; J.D. told the *Oklahoman*, "We used that trip to look at how they started, what beers they started with and what size system because we needed to figure out where we need to be as a start up in this market and meet the production needs of what we think demand will be." A manual seven-barrel brewhouse with four seven-barrel fermenters and two fifteen-barrel fermenters was the initial setup, all powered by an up-and-coming Wind Credit Program through Oklahoma Gas and Electric. In an effort to be eco-conscious, they donated their spent grain to a partnership with the Oklahoma Farmers Cooperative and explored ways to conserve water.

A Handcrafted History

COOP Ale Works' original brewhouse. *Courtesy of COOP Ale Works.*

Located originally at 1124 Northwest Fifty-First in Oklahoma City, the distribution-only microbrewery had immediate interest from its neighbor, the 51st Street Speakeasy club. Owner Kevin Sine jumped on the opportunity to serve as a makeshift taproom for folks to sample the newest brewery to hit the city. "On specific days we'd have an open house for people to come see the brewery and then give them a coupon to go next door and sample our beers," said Merryweather. The brewpub circuit was heavily inundated, and to make the styles of beer they wanted, a distribution brewery was their only option. March 1, 2009, saw the first keg sales to local bars and restaurants, with initial offerings of Horny Toad, a cerveza-style ale; Native Amber, a malty amber ale; and DNR, or Do Not Resuscitate, a 10 percent Belgian strong golden ale that was the first of its kind to be brewed in Oklahoma. Zeppelin, a German wheat ale, was based on a beer Chase had brewed for his wedding. While the snappy clove flavor was very favorable, the group decided to tone it down for the mass market. "Everyone liked it but we thought the heavy clove flavor would be too dominant for the public's palate, so we scaled it back to where it had a milder coriander taste. (The name would eventually be changed to

Elevator Wheat after a name dispute with another brewery.) Gran Sport Porter, which featured a Vespa scooter on the label commemorating J.D.'s tenure as president of the Vespa Club of America, was soon added to round out the core lineup. For their first fall and winter season, Chase brewed Territorial Reserve Oak Aged Imperial Stout, an Oktoberfest beer and an oak barrel–aged imperial stout that spent time in Bulleit bourbon barrels. J.D. served as the marketing director out of the gate, armed with his wit and passion for good beer. A graduate from Webster University St. Louis and a longtime commercial photographer originally from Akron, Ohio, J.D. enjoyed the aspects of high-quality craftsmanship when it came to photography. After losing out on a job thanks to the increasing popularity of color film, family ties brought him to Oklahoma, where he landed a job in commercial photography and construction. With a competitive and aggressive mindset, the crew were determined to be the top producing brewery in the state. "At the time, I was thinking Native Amber would be our flagship beer but Horny Toad won out with its approachability in a young, immature beer market," said J.D. Their amber beer was their hoppiest offering when it was first brewed. In the summer of 2010, sixteen-ounce cans of Horny Toad and Native Amber hit liquor store shelves. "The choice of cans was very important to us because of the recyclability," said Merryweather.

Soon fans came to them asking for an IPA. A plan was in the making for a top-quality IPA, but they did not want to rush anything too soon to market. As so happens, Blake Jarolim, a teacher and avid homebrewer, met Chase and other likeminded beer enthusiasts through tasting groups. "I had the summer off being a teacher, and Chase needed help at COOP and asked if I wanted to come work at the brewery part time," recalled Blake. The answer was a no-brainer and would eventually lead the two to collaborate and brew what is now known as F5 IPA. Originally slated as a seasonal beer, F5 won over many fans early, prompting the brewery to keep it year round. "At the time we developed a bitter, West Coast–style IPA that was super popular in the market," said Blake. Both brewed two to three test batches around the same concept with slightly different hop varieties. "I think I brewed two of them and Blake brewed three. We kinda picked the one we liked best and that's what we went with. I'm sure it was probably his—Blake's a good brewer," said Chase modestly to Nick Trougakos. However, the first time Blake brewed was almost his last. "I thought, why am I doing this? It'd be just as easy to go to a liquor store and buy a six-pack." After the unfavorable waft of boiling malt and hops died down, he noticed the miraculous

Horny Toad packaging. *Courtesy of COOP Ale Works.*

transformation going on in his fermentation bucket the next day. "I noticed all the little bubbles coming up and that was the hook in my mouth that something was happening and I wasn't even touching it," said Blake.

With more than sixty accounts in restaurants and bars, COOP made waves within its first year. Packaging was moved to the summer of 2010 because demand was so high for keg sales. Word of mouth, early adoption to social media channels and beer dinners at local restaurants helped fuel sales in a very new market for craft beer. Its first-year anniversary grew to be a big annual tradition as a thank-you to the fans who supported the brewery from the beginning. Oklahoma City, known as Boom Town, was seeing a revolution around 2011 in small-scale entrepreneurs building up a culture of local artisans like COOP, local coffee roaster Elemental Coffee and Ludivine, a farm-to-fork restaurant. As happenstance goes, these three entities formed a relationship and one night hashed out a concept that J.D. had seen in his world travels of night markets. The area of Hudson and Eighth Streets was blossoming, and they felt that this area was perfect to set up some food trucks, sell some beer and increase the quality of life for Oklahomans. However, the first food truck event, dubbed H&8th, barely got

COOP Ale Works' one-year anniversary party. *Courtesy of COOP Ale Works.*

started, as it was shut down by city inspectors and ABLE agents "armed with badges and guns." "Discussions quickly ensued and a lot of publicity that did not bode well for the raid party stirred a surge of interest and support for the food trucks, and the next H&8th was a hit," reported *Oklahoman* writer Steve Lackmeyer. It instilled economic energy in downtown Oklahoma City, bringing people together unlike any other time before. Music acts, poetry readings and pop-up shops soon followed this festival, which took place monthly from spring to fall. COOP used this opportunity to create a line of sessionable beers that could be sold at events just like this and used H&8th as a testing ground. One year it made $34,000 in four hours from beer sales.

The brewery scaled up fast, and J.D. moved into a full-time position as sales and marketing director. In another big change, Blake moved into the brewmaster role. Co-founder Mark Seibold released this statement at the time:

> *We met Blake Jarolim at the first social rave in February 2009 before we opened our doors. Blake started out a fan of COOP, and I quickly learned that his brewing prowess was matched with passion and unbound energy.*

A Handcrafted History

It's great to talk about all the nerdy-technical aspects of brewing with Blake because he is so attuned to detail, having brewed literally every style of beer known to man. Blake's knowledge of brewing is unparalleled, and I think Oklahoma City is going to be surprised with what we have planned in the next year or so.

In 2012, they were selected to pour DNR and Native Amber at SAVOR, a high-end craft beer and food pairing event in Washington, D.C. Through the next few years, COOP settled in as Oklahoma City's brewery, being the largest producer of craft beer at the time. After the release of F5 in April 2010, it dominated sales by almost 50 percent, beating out its two flagship beers. However, it wasn't offered in cans until August 2013. "Releasing our best-selling draft beer in a can has been in our plans for more than a year," said J.D. "Our production capabilities have recently been expanded with the purchase of two new fermenters and the addition of a new state of the art canning system. F5 IPA is one of the highest rated IPAs in the region, and Oklahomans continue to surprise us by their insatiable demand for this beer." Another milestone was being the first Oklahoma brewery to commercially brew a sour beer, known as COOP Farmhouse Ale. Blake laid out their reasons to the *Thirsty Beagle* blog: "Our Farmhouse Ale was a small batch attempt to provide Oklahoma with the type of beer that has trouble making it across our borders. We fermented this beer with a normal ale yeast and then inoculated it with a wild yeast/bacteria slurry that was cultured in the brewery. It aged for a couple of months before we added 40 lbs of tart cherries and let it age for a few more months. When it reached an appropriate level of tartness, we kegged it, tried it, and loved it!"

Business was booming, and COOP knew that it needed to scale up. In November 2013, it signed a seven-year lease for a new 14,400-square-foot building near Council Road and State Highway 152 in southwest Oklahoma City. The building was equipped with a new fully automated thirty-barrel brewhouse along with 10,000 extra square feet for expansion. This allowed its team of six full-time employees to ramp up production and eventually offer all six of its year-round beers in cans by the summer of 2014. Increased production also saw the opportunity to expand into new markets like Missouri, Kansas and north Texas. Although the tasting bill had passed, COOP was not fully ready to open its doors to patrons. Its efforts as a full distribution brewery had kept it from providing small-batch beers to test with the local market. Eventually, it carved out a space in its facility next to the cold room storage to allow people to come in and sample experimental beers.

Head brewer Blake Jarolim poses next to his pilot system at COOP Ale Works. *Photo by the author.*

Thanks to the success and sweat equity put into events like H&8th, COOP developed three new beers to cater to the grocery and convenience store consumers. These establishments were only allowed to carry 3.2 percent ABW beer, and festivals only allowed sales of these beers to the public. "We've spent 26 months developing and testing these three beers with the intent to release them once we relocated to our new facility and caught up with demand for our primary offerings," Blake Jarolim told the *Oklahoman*. "We've seen a huge and growing demand for lighter craft beers with unique and distinctive flavor profiles, and we spent a lot of time perfecting these recipes, none of which sacrifice their flavor for the lower alcohol content." Originally produced in a four-pack of sixteen-ounce cans, Briefcase Brown; Negative Split, a Belgian-style table beer; and its most popular seller, Spare Rib Pale Ale, debuted in November 2014 as the biggest offering of craft cans Oklahoma had ever seen in the market at that time. "We're really looking forward to expanding our presence in Oklahoma and growing presence with hundreds of new venues," said J.D.

COOP continued to make wise investments by evaluating the market each year and slipping into trends on its own terms. Its emphasis on quality control was key to the development of consistent products with its on-site lab. No one person ever took credit for the creation of a beer—it was a collaborative effort. Internal investment was key, with onboarding staff that cared about the product and COOP offering yearly stipends to back them up, be it trips to the Craft Brewers Conference or Great American Beer Festival to instill the culture of craft beer. "You have to remember, there aren't a lot of opportunities locally to inculturate our employees and understand the industry from the inside," said Blake. COOP stretched its legs a bit in 2017 with a line of beers based on the popular DNR known as the Casket Series. Brandy Barrel Cherry DNR was the first 375ml cork and caged bottle in the series, with DNR sitting in barrels for more than a year. On filling gaps in their portfolio, Blake mentioned, "We are always analyzing our sales figures on a year to year basis and production capacity is utilized in the best possible way and to minimize stale beer on the shelf." It was a constant battle of space and constraints, but nothing new to a fledgling brewery that built up a niche market and opened the doors for so many others that followed.

BATTERED BOAR BREWING (2009–PRESENT)

"Good beers will fight to survive." This is just one of many quotes that have come from one of Oklahoma's earliest craft breweries. Mike Sandefur's background was in combative arts as a tactical weapons instructor for roughly twenty years. "I had a student that was a glass half empty sort of guy, a pleasant fellow but just a pessimistic view on the world. I tried my best to show him the beautiful things in life like a baker that makes his own bread or a brewer that makes his own beer. My brother-in-law bought me a homebrewing kit that sat in the garage and never got used. I take this guy to the Brew Shop in OKC to brew some beer and lift this guy's spirit up." In taking on this endeavor, Mike was rewarded with the new hobby of homebrewing. This story displays Mike's generous persona and his philosophies on brewing. In his first year, he recalled brewing at least two hundred batches of beer with a very curious nature. As a child, he remembered watching cooking shows with his mom and took to cooking at home at a very young age. He was born and raised in downtown Edmond, Oklahoma, but there was not a lot of information and resources for brewers in the late 2000s. Mike let his curiosity feed his desire to learn more.

Mike started reading up on what he could find with homebrewing books, and eventually "every flat surface in my home had a fermenter sitting on it," as his wife jokingly told him. While it was good for a laugh, she gave an ultimatum to get serious about brewing and stop filling the house with fermenters. With the assistance from a former ABLE attorney, Mike started up Battered Boar Brewing Company in 2008. But where did such a name come about? In the sweltering July heat of 1998, Mike went on a wild boar hunt with only a knife. He had been on several hunting trips before as a youngster and wanted to experience something new since he never knew of anyone else who had done it. Now, over time, the boar seemed to grow to monstrous sizes, depending on who you talked to. But Mike will tell you that it was a 480-pound Russian boar that he killed with a knife. So, when it came time to name his brewery, he figured it was a crazy enough name with a cheeky backstory to grab general interest in his beer.

"Just because we can, doesn't mean we should," quipped Mike as we discussed the eclectic beers he produced over the years. Every brewer has his or her stance on the world and a different palate they like to use to express those views. With Mike's culinary sensibility in his arsenal, Battered Boar pulled off some ambitious recipes right out of the gate. As he sees it, there's an equal chance to fail as to succeed, and when they do succeed, it can elevate the art of brewing. He also believes that just because others are making a successful beer or using another ingredient, it doesn't mean they have to follow the trend. After meeting with Sam Calagionne at a craft brewers conference early in his career, he took away some advice that he holds dear to this day. "Sam told me if you can clearly articulate your vision and adequately reproduce your beers then the skies are the limit." While he is fully aware of what everyone around him is brewing, it doesn't shape his opinion on what he wants to serve at his brewery.

With his vision in place, Mike came upon some seed money in the most peculiar way from a nationally touring artist who wanted to train with Mike. Chris Gaylor, drummer for the All-American Rejects, came to train a few months later and eventually invested in the brewery to help them get started. As of 2012 or so, he parted ways, but they remained good friends. A five-barrel brewhouse was soon up and running in a small industrial area of Edmond. The entire brewery and bottling line was pieced together by Mike and his friends. "When we started in 2009 we'd brew about 5 bbls a day, 5 days a week, and most of it for production at the time because we couldn't sell out the door yet," recalled Mike. Over time, they added more fermentation tanks to keep up with production. In the beginning, their three core beers—Company Man Pale Ale, Briar Patch Amber Ale and Heartbreak Hefeweizen—were distributed throughout Oklahoma. However, distribution was not the best, and Mike learned early on that his product was going bad on the shelves, which in turn gave his brewery a negative image. He redirected courses and started to distribute them into Arkansas, Georgia and Texas for about eighteen months because of inconsistent wholesale practices in Oklahoma.

A Handcrafted History

Battered Boar Brewing's flagship beers. *From the* Oklahoman.

Early on, they started with eclectic beers like the Coconut Cream Stout, which was loaded down with lots of chocolate malt and loads of coconut; to this day, it outsells most of their beers. Mike reached out to the Stratford Peach Festival right before it opened and proposed to make a fresh peach ale to be the official beer of the festival. What sounded like a grand marketing idea was eventually a waste of time because Stratford was in a dry county—another slight on the times and restrictions that breweries faced. Another popular beer featured the aforementioned Chuck Deveney of the Brew Shop, as his likeness was put onto a pumpkin for Chuck's Pumpkin Ale. "Unfortunately, Chuck didn't have any input on the beer," recalled Mike. "I just wanted to name a beer after him and he did contribute his likeness." One poked fun at the movie *Braveheart* but contained a serious beer inside the bottle. Blue Face Scottish Ale, in Mike's opinion, was the best beer they produced and one he's most proud of creating. "It's just one of those bulletproof beers and a Scottish ale is what I started out with when I first got started brewing. It's an underrepresented style and for us, it was a culmination of technique and time to get it to taste the way we wanted." In regards to their core beers, Mike admitted it was certainly a formulaic process of developing approachable, easy-drinking beers like an IPA, amber or an American wheat beer. It certainly worked, as he and a small crew met distribution demands without a taproom in which to serve beer. By the time legislation allowed taprooms to serve samples of beer, Mike was completely against it. He did not want to essentially scale down his product, which was selling well enough on the shelves. After about three years in, they moved across the street and nearly doubled in size, this time building an area for a taproom with the anticipation of legislation changing in the near future.

Mike's son, Jordan, started brewing with his dad in 2006 with the same passion and fervor. "He's dogmatic and inflexible about the quality of his work and I couldn't be more proud of him. Obviously, he's my son, but take that away, he's still unbelievable," said Mike. It was especially helpful as time marched on, and other limited-release beers were bottled, like La Padite, a farmhouse ale with Galaxy hops, fruit and spices, or Chocolate Cherry Porter, brewed with Ocumare chocolate, vanilla and sweet bing cherries. There was also Lion's Tooth Floret, a farmhouse ale brewed with dandelions; Dante's Porter, brewed with peppers; and an American wheat beer that was dry-hopped named Ultimo Hombre. Once the laws changed in Oklahoma to allow taprooms to serve high-point beer on site, Mike's world completely opened up. Gone were the dreaded days of depending solely on distribution to survive in the industry. "We make a beer now called Lime Saltun. It's a farmhouse beer weighing in at 8.5 percent brewed with key lines and Cyprus sea salt. If there was a metaphor for what we do and encapsulate Battered Boar in a flavor, it might be this one. It's very fresh and never more than forty-eight hours old. It's a simple product that uses the best ingredients on the planet, period. We use Hawaiian-grown key limes and Cyprus sea salt from the Mediterranean, and it just shows us what can be done with simple ingredients and the best we can do."

For the past dozen years, Battered Boar continues to unapologetically make beers that stand the test of time when it knows it put in the best ingredients and has a commitment to take time in planning out every conceivable detail, bringing the customer back for more. Being the quotable man that Mike is, he'll likely tell you, "Beers are born out of passion and necessity." The passion had always been there, with a desire to run a successful business despite restrictions. "The necessity comes into play when we can't not make a beer. The beer won't leave me alone and that's part of our measuring stick. Everyone gets ideas, but it needs to stand up to our standards and everyone that comes through our doors. Nobody smiles at a bad beer, so we strive to get the look of satisfaction and smile from our customers with every beer we make." And you can quote him on that.

Mustang Brewing (2009–2017)

Working in the corporate structure of a large healthcare system, native Oklahoman Tim Schoelen had always wanted to flex his entrepreneurial muscles. Inspired by his father, who was an avid homebrewer, Tim took an interest after tasting a Belgian-style witbier his dad brewed. The thought stewed with him as he and his wife took note of all the local breweries they would visit while traveling for work. His business neurons started firing, and he thought that his dad could start a whole brewery based on his beers. However, his father wanted to keep it a hobby, knowing full well the tremendous task it would take to create a full-scale brewery. What would be the harm in writing up a business plan, thought Tim. So, he did just that; he pooled together some friends to raise about $75,000 in capital, sold his home, cashed out his and his wife's 401(k), moved into a rental home and taught himself how to make beer in his garage in Bethany, Oklahoma. "I didn't learn how to make beer because I love beer; I learned how to brew beer to start a brewery"—a different mindset, but one that was not alone in the early 2008 boom of craft breweries being opened every week across America.

As a drinker of lawnmower beers and a self-acclaimed "Old Style" drinker, Tim brewed some wild beers for his friends to try, with not many passing the taste test. "We eventually came up with some gateway beers that bridged the gap from Coors drinkers to show how local breweries can make a similar and better product in their backyard," said Tim. In a heavily populated area of macro-beer drinkers, Tim had quite the endeavor ahead of him. "I would always get asked, 'What's your lightest beer?' and you know what that tells me is that I have one chance to convert that person. Now I love IPAs and milk stouts, but you can't hand that to someone who hasn't ventured beyond light beers—they'll likely never try craft beer again." So, his philosophy of brewing was to brew lighter, easy-drinking beers and engage the public in a discussion of what craft beer can be and how there is a story behind every beer brewed. The craft beer movement had come to a tipping point and had finally made its way, like the wind sweeping through the plains of Oklahoma.

Tim started developing beer recipes out of his garage. After visiting his family in St. Louis, Missouri, over the years, he learned about O'Fallon Brewing Company and its contract beer services. Once that was established and they started to brew their flagship beer, the Golden Ale, the bottling procedure took place in Stevens Point, Wisconsin. The beer's authenticity came under fire early on when consumers learned that an Oklahoma beer was brewed and packaged in other states. Contract brewing had a poor stigma that has since been quelled with the popularity of gypsy brewers. Naturally, it took time to ramp up capital and promote the product at local and regional craft beer festivals. Relying on a contract brewing method was tiresome, and Tim found a new brewmaster early on. Enter award-winning homebrewer Gary Shellman.

Gary was stationed overseas in the military in the early 1980s, and upon his arrival back to the States, he was soon on the hunt for good beer. Around 1989, Gary was introduced to homebrewing from a friend using the simplest method of extract brewing. He honed his skills for the next ten years, brewing a variety of styles; in 1999, he was introduced to Bob Carbony and made his first all-grain beer. Bob was a legend in the homebrewing circuit, winning Brewer of the Year in 2002 and the Bluebonnet HomeBrewer Competition held in Texas. Gary continued his tutelage under Bob, with improved procedures like temperature control, up until 2008, when he was introduced to Tim. "I had volunteered to pour beer at a few festivals and I invited him out to my house to try my beers. At the time I had about 14 different beers kegged and I pestered him for about 3–4 months to come out and try some. Finally he told me if he came out there, it'd be a likely trip to the ER afterwards." Tim countered Gary's offer with a challenge. Tim told him, "If you're as good as everyone says you are, I'll give you the recipe to Mustang Golden Ale and we'll do a blind taste test of our kegs and bottles against your version." So, Gary went to work, and after four weeks, he was ready in January 2009. A blind taste test resulted with four of the five judges choosing Gary's beer as the production Golden Ale. Tim turned to his wife and said, "I think we found our new brewmaster." Eventually, they served their first pint of Golden Ale on July 13, 2009, at McNellie's Pub in Oklahoma City.

Mustang profited well with its decision, as Gary went on to make an award-winning beer right from the start. As told to Nick Trougakos of the *Oklahoman*:

A Handcrafted History

Washita Wheat has a very distinct but mild fruitiness. The use of red wheat relates back to olden days when that was the primary wheat source in Oklahoma (and the rest of America). There was a departure from Red Wheat to White Wheat, and many breweries use white wheat in their recipes today. Using red wheat is more traditional, and has a smoothness you just can't get any other way. Six years ago I stopped by a field in Chickasha one evening and discussed harvesting, food and beer with a local crew. I agreed to bring five gallons of beer the following night to use as trade for some of their red wheat. We cooked porterhouse steaks on the grill, right there in the field, drank some home brew, and I drove home with 30 lbs of red wheat. I started using it in one of my wheat beer recipes, and, thus, Washita Wheat was born.

The beer took home a silver medal in 2010 and a gold medal in 2011 at the World Beer Championships in Chicago, Illinois. Their second seasonal, Harvest Lager, also took home a silver medal in 2010 and a bronze medal in 2011. The exposure resonated, with more than fifty-five thousand cases of beer sold throughout Oklahoma in 2012, with even more in Kansas and Arkansas. Mustang's Winter Lager, also a gold medalist, was so popular it brought it back as a year-round beer and renamed it Route 66 American Lager. All in all, Mustang collected ten medals with its beers in the early stages of production. It released both beers in twelve-packs of cans just in time for summer of 2011.

Mustang developed several lines of beers: a Heritage line with its easy-drinking year-round lineup, a sessionable series with Mustang '33 and then

Mustang Brewing Company's brewhouse.
Photo by the author.

a barrel-aged Saddlebag Series for the diverse beer scene developing in Oklahoma City. The '33 session ale, brewed similar to a kolsch-style ale with three types of barley and German Hallertau hops, was made for consumers who liked to shop at grocery and convenience stores and could only buy 3.2 ABW beer. Tim admitted that he wasn't the biggest fan of canned beer, and most of their limited barrel-aged beers were bottled in large bomber bottles and transitioned to four- and six-packs. A big imperial stout from Gary's arsenal was Brandy's Barrel Sundae, an imperial porter with vanilla and aged in brandy barrels. Other beers in the series included a Russian-style Imperial Court Stout infused with raspberries and Dragon's Breath, an ale brewed with chili peppers, released every quarter with unique label art from local concert poster artist Thom Self.

Tim worked on bringing production to Oklahoma to have a better handle on recipe development and keg production for local accounts. The OKCity Brewing Cooperative, a facility that had come online in 2011 at 1354 West Sheridan Avenue, made a deal with Mustang to take over its operation in the fall of 2012. "This will be a gradual process," Mustang brewmaster Gary Shellman told the *Oklahoman*. "Bringing all keg production in-house is step one. Step two will be expanding capacity and adding a bottling and canning line that can accommodate our growing production needs." Its first beer brewed in Oklahoma was the Pawnee Pale Ale, released in March 2011. Tim also wanted to embrace the up-and-coming brewers by giving them a space to start without all the upfront costs, just like Mustang's origins. "We plan to further expand the cooperative aspect by bulk-buying materials we share, such as base grain, packaging and chemicals and ultimately sharing in the savings," said Tim. Before Mustang could even move into the facility, Tim received a text message from Taylor Hanson of the Hanson brothers music trio. "I'm not quite sure the reason why they reached out, but at the time we were doing a lot of marketing with local musicians and they wanted to come and try their hand at brewing," recalled Tim. What started as a hobby turned into a wildly popular beer and music movement.

Mustang operated the facility with three other tenants until one fateful day on May 31, 2013, when an F3 tornado struck the area and devastated the new facility. It took all but eight seconds to dismantle the roof and destroy the steel fermenters beyond repair, along with the hundreds of gallons of beer inside. "We'll be able to use one 15 bbl tank out of the 10 brewing vessels that were operational, including the mash tun and boil kettle," said Gary to the *Tulsa World*. Operations ceased for about five months, and luckily, Mustang had its other contract brewing running to keep up with distribution. "We luckily had just delivered two to three-months' supply to distributors in Oklahoma earlier in the week," Schoelen told the *Oklahoman*. Tim had been working on an effort for a new space, with offices, a warehouse, a taproom and a green room for traveling musicians who performed at the brewery. The twelve-thousand-square-foot facility was just down the road off Meridian Avenue and housed a seven-barrel brew system with three thirty-barrel fermenters. Bottling of their year-round beers was soon contracted out to their friends at Krebs, and the new space was ready to open on November 1, to coincide with the passing of the new beer sampling legislation.

After reorganizing under a new location and with the cooperative now shut down, Mustang focused on its session beers to serve in its new taproom. However, the tornado had marked the beginning of the end, as it continued on with production at a much slower pace. While it had done its best to sponsor local events, boost the local music scene and get its beer out into the masses, there was more lurking behind the scenes that led to its closing. The new brewhouse was smaller and unable to keep up with demand for the developing beer scene. At a time when Mustang should have been all in, it was barely keeping up with keg production. While it excelled at bringing beer into the market with lower upfront costs, it would eventually catch up with it due to high shipping costs, sending its brewmaster to Wisconsin for quality assurance and the rising costs of ingredients. It was losing money on every case produced, which could not be sustained in any business practice despite a new taproom and legislation that allowed it to serve high-strength beers in 2016.

By the summer of 2015, Gary had decided to retire after six and a half years of being brewmaster. At this time, Elk Valley brewing had begun operations alongside legendary brewer Mike Groshong, who took over as brewmaster when Gary left. About one year later, on July 30, 2016, Tim announced that he would be stepping down and sold off his stake to local oil and gas investor Scott White. Mr. White, along with other oil investors, had big plans of moving the brewery north to Edmond, with the possibility of continuing the cooperative business model. Plans also included a full restaurant, a music venue and one hundred taps to serve the budding area of Edmond and north OKC. Unfortunately, the grand scheme had fizzled out by 2017, when he announced that he'd shutter the business that summer after the passing of his father. The facility remained dormant until Brad Stumph, an original member of the brewing cooperative, founded the Brewers Union in 2018 to rekindle the start-up business model once again.

Redbud Brewing Company (2010–2013)

"I knew if I took the conventional route: find a property, seek financing, purchase equipment and build a brewery, it would be a year or more before I would be making beer again," Chase Healey told the *Southwest Brewing News*. As former head brewer of COOP, Chase set out on his own as a self-described "gypsy brewer" to make unique beers he couldn't produce at a traditional brewery. "I helped grow the Oklahoma City beer scene, and I still wanted to be a part of it." His options of where to brew were limited. He called up his friend Rick Huebert, the first post-Prohibition microbrewery owner in the state, and said, "I took him to lunch, told him what I had in mind, and he was completely supportive." He brewed under the moniker Redbud Brewing in homage to the state tree of Oklahoma. With that, he got to work and created a session beer known as Redbud Pale Ale, clocking in at 5.4 percent ABV and 30 IBUs; it garnered good reviews on the website RateBeer, like this one from user "troyc": "Pours a reddish amber color with a slight haze to it. Very little head. Pronounced hoppy aroma of pine and spruce needles as well as some light citrus. Tangy citrus fruit notes mix well with the pine. Caramel and bread notes are there, but take a back seat in the flavor department. Pleasant mouthfeel and carbonation levels. Some alcohol is perceived in the finish." Initial offerings were in kegs to local bars and restaurants, with the intent to fill twelve-ounce bottles.

Then came a line of beers that really challenged the perception of unique flavor profiles. They were known as the Cuvee Series, where each beer was a blend of the previous and brewed in limited quantities that could not be replicated. Cuvee 1 was a Belgian Golden Ale with sugary, tart fruit flavors with spice notes. "Cuvee 2 will be a barrel age version of 1 and Cuvee 3 will be a blend of 1 and a new beer." When asked about his brewing methods, Healey responded, "This is my craft, the beers are my artistic expressions. I want to add something unique to not just Oklahoma beer but craft beer as a whole." He certainly did that as he outgrew his space at Huebert's and struck up a deal with a new enterprise that was gaining traction all around the country.

OKCity Brewing Cooperative (2012–2013)

"The growth in craft beer has shown everyone that the drinking populace wants options when it comes to beer," Greg Powell, manager of Tapwerks, told Nick Trougakos. "It has also shown us that a city our size is large enough to support more than just a handful of breweries." Housed in an inconspicuous building were gleaming tanks and a brewhouse that would give several breweries a chance to start their dream. Sibyl Kang opened in April 2012 with the intent to give fledgling breweries in Oklahoma a spot to create and bring beer to market at a fraction of the upfront costs. Her first tenant was Redbud Brewing, as Chase had outgrown his space at Huebert's and needed more room to experiment with his barrel-aged Cuvee series. In May, Anthem Brewing joined on, and Black Mesa followed as the third brewery in July. "It's a great arrangement," said Brad Stumph of Black Mesa. "OKCity Brewing acts as a brewery incubator, and we have a way to contribute to all that is happening in the Oklahoma craft beer scene much sooner than if we had had to build our own brewery first." The concept was simple: brewers rented time to brew to produce beers quickly and bring in capital faster. Most started with kegs for draft accounts, as a bottling line was in the works. Another benefit was being able to lean on one another for tips, techniques and advice, which created a rich culture of brewing in Oklahoma. "A lot of the stuff that we're trying to do in there, beyond our more standard lineup, is stuff that we're experimenting and trying things," Healey said. "It's always nice to have a fellow brewer to ask a question or two about techniques and ways to get the best results. We are there to help one another and support one another."

In August, their first tenant decided to pursue a different venture. Chase left the Redbud brand behind, along with several unmarked barrels filled with hundreds of gallons of beer, for a new venture in Texas. Sibyl announced that she would hire a new brewer to continue the program, yet that never came to fruition. By November, the company had taken a big turn, and Mustang Brewing purchased the business along with the Redbud brand and recipes. "I have enjoyed learning the craft brewing business and want to see it continue to grow," Kang said. "I believe everything happens for a reason and when the opportunity presented itself we knew

Cuvee Series from Redbud Brewing Company. *Photo by Scot Poland.*

Mustang Brewing Company brewmaster Gary Shellman (*left*), getting the mash tank ready to brew beer at OKCity Brewing Cooperative in Oklahoma City, February 6, 2013. *Photo by Paul B. Southerland, from the* Oklahoman.

it was the right thing to do at the right time. I think Mustang will be able to take it to the next level and continue what has been started." Mustang had been searching to bring its brewing operations to Oklahoma, and this seemed like the best time. "Moving our brewing operations in-house has always been the plan, it was just a matter of finding the best situation for the company," Mustang president Tim Schoelen said. "We are extremely excited to enter into this phase of our business plan." Initial plans were to have all Mustang beer kegged out of the co-op and produce some of its Saddlebag Series beers as well with a new bottling and canning line.

As for the Redbud brand, Mustang had planned on using the line as a new start in creating artisanal beers that were opposite of the session styles for which it was known. Then disaster struck. On May 31, in just eight short seconds, the co-op was hit by a tornado that lifted the roof up and slammed it back down, rendering all but one fermentation vessel useless and spelling the end of the co-op. Black Mesa lost nearly 1,400 gallons of beer, although Anthem, which had most of its beer already in distribution, skated by without any losses. They both forged their own paths, leading to a new wave of microbreweries in the state.

A Handcrafted History

Hanson Brothers Brewing Company (2013–Present)

"I remember receiving a text message from Taylor Hanson one day about possibly brewing a beer for them, and the rest was history," recalled Tim Schoelen of Mustang Brewing. Mustang had incorporated itself as a proponent for local music since its inception, and this enticed the Hanson brothers to create a beer for themselves. All throughout their years of touring, they had encountered beer styles from around the world and thought it would be ideal to have one for themselves. Many bands found ways to merchandise and create bonds with their fans and were discovering the world of craft beer right alongside them. "The fans literally have grown up with us," said Taylor Hanson. They reached out to Mustang around 2012 to create a signature beer. With the help of brewmaster Gary Shellman, they turned out a tasty citrus-forward flavored beer with a small hop finish that was aptly named Mmmhops. The trio released the beer around the Los Angeles premiere of *The Hangover: Part III*, in which their iconic song "Mmmbop" was featured. The brew won a gold medal from the Beverage Tasting Institute in 2014 and by 2015 was available for sale in sixteen states, including Florida, where you could purchase it at Disney's Epcot Center.

The beer spurred a music and craft beer festival called the Hop Jam, which debuted on May 22, 2014, in the Brady Arts District of Tulsa. Their very first performance was in 1992 at the famous Mayfest Arts Festival, and this was a fitting way to draw attention to the town that raised them. Craft breweries from the state and surrounding region came to showcase their beers, with a free live concert provided by several bands and, of course, Hanson. "With Tulsa we feel like we want to do more special stuff in our hometown," Taylor Hanson told the *Tulsa World*. "If we are going to do a show, let's do a big outside free show that everybody can come to and that is different from any other show we're doing on a tour." Their second beer, a spiced farmhouse saison dubbed Hop Jam Festive Ale, was developed at Mustang's new facility after the tornado of May 2013 demolished the original facility. "It's going to have a classic Saison spice with a little pepper and hoppy at the end, so it will have some bitterness from the hops," Taylor told Tom Gilbert of the *Tulsa World*. "This is a beer for people really into the traditional styles and stuff that is less common, something that is really different." The recipe included a light barley malt base with two-row and melanoidin and rye malt for a touch of spice. The farmhouse yeast gave it a light smokiness and citrus fragrance to the beer that debuted in 750ml bombers and on draft at the 2014 Hop Jam.

After Mustang closed its doors in 2017, Hanson needed a new home to brew their beer. A young brewery in Tulsa had just started up in 2015 and was ready for the challenge. Dead Armadillo Brewing was familiar with the contract brewing business model when it first started brewing its amber ale at Roughtail Brewing. Mmmhops had transitioned to cans for easier access and wider distribution. They eventually moved their spiced farmhouse ale into cans as well. They would soon collaborate on a beer released in bombers called Inland Porter, named after the Port of Catoosa near Tulsa. Over the years, they have continued to release special beers at the Hop Jam, including a collaboration beer with Destihl Brewing Company called Pink Moonlight Peach Milkshake IPA, Second Breakfast Imperial Stout and a saison with blueberries in 2019. Collaborations like these occurred as Hanson toured the country and invited breweries to the Hop Jam. Destihl shared their love of beer and music, as the head brewer played with the band at GABF in 2014. Each year, they created stronger connections with special events like the Brewers' Table Dinner, which featured celebrity brewers like Sam Calagione of Dogfish Head, Chad Yakobson of Crooked Stave, Chris Rigoulot of Noble Rey and local brewmaster Eric Marshall of Marshall Brewing and raised funds for the Community Food Bank. In 2017, they debuted two more special-release beers. Redland, an amber ale brewed with "roasted American and British grain, balanced by a medley of floral hops," was named for the red dirt prominently found in Oklahoma. Tulsa Tea, an imperial stout, "includes eight different grains plus flaked oats, cocoa nibs and a trio of hops and the complex roasted flavor profile includes strong chocolate and subtle coffee undertones, hints of bourbon and vanilla, and finishes with a spicy hop bitterness and pointed nose." Other interactions included beer tastings and a Hop Talks discussion panel with Oklahoma brewers. In 2019, more than one hundred breweries were represented, making it the largest craft beer festival held in Oklahoma.

Black Mesa Brewing (2012–Present)

"About seven years before I retired from the Midwest City Fire Department I started homebrewing and really enjoyed it. Especially the recipe development portion. So when I retired I wanted to start a second career and brewing seemed a natural fit." Chris Sanders honed his craft for about twenty years

A Handcrafted History

and furthered his education at the Master Brewers Association in Madison, Wisconsin. He later earned his brewing certificate at the Institute of Brewing and Distilling in London. With these newly developed skills, Chris joined up with Huebert Brewing in 2009 as Rick was looking for more assistance to keep up with his heavy brew schedule. "I helped Rick upgrade his bottling line and change the labeling system to make it more streamlined," Chris recalled. Over the next few years, Chris expanded Huebert's offerings to include the Wild Pony Wheat, Tucker Pale Ale, Rasenmaher (a German-style kolsch) and Deep Deuce Porter. Life was good and Chris was looking to strike out on his own. At the time, Sibyl Kang had started up the OKCity Brewing Cooperative in Oklahoma City. This was the perfect opportunity for Chris to try out some recipes he had tucked away and formulate his own brewery. As if the universe was listening in, a wildlife biologist by the name of Brad Stumph stopped by one day. "Brad came around Huebert's curious of the brewing scene, and we hit it off after I gave him a tour of the place. I reached out to him not long after. I'm more on the brewing side and needed someone to help with sales and the business end of the brewery and that's how we got started," Chris recalled.

Chris Sanders contract brewing at O'Fallon Brewing Company. *Courtesy of Black Mesa Brewing Company.*

They named their brewery after the state's highest point, Black Mesa, which rests in western Oklahoma. Brad, an experienced climber, was on track to traverse the highest points in each state when he stopped in Oklahoma. Chris's time at the cooperative was inspiring, as there were two other brewers to bounce ideas off of one another from time to time. "While we were there we brewed our Blonde ale that was as true to a Kolsch as I could get. We decided to call it Blonde since most Americans would be familiar with that style. Later we changed it to Kolsch and decided to educate the consumer," Chris told me. His philosophy for brewing was to bring old-world styles back to Oklahoma with his unique twist on them. The pace was good as they started in August 2012, but fate would have another path. On May 31, the El Reno F3 tornado devastated the area and lifted the roof off the OKCity Brewing complex. It was just enough to damage most of the brewing equipment, although luckily it struck when no one was inside.

"We lost 6 months of brewing after the tornado hit," recalled Chris. He decided to spend those days on his homebrew system and tweak recipes while they decided on the next step. "We started to circle outside and talked to other breweries. We found O'Fallon Brewing in O'Fallon, Missouri, and got to talking with Brian Owens, their head brewer at the time. We just talked the same talk and had a really good rapport as far as philosophy and brewing style." Contract brewing carried a stigma in the early 2000s among craft purists, but people soon realized that with transparency these breweries just wanted to make their dream a reality. "Many were sympathetic with our story since the tornado hit."

The second beer he produced at the cooperative was Endless Skyway Bitter. The name referenced local musician Woody Guthrie's song "This Land Is Your Land." Chris Whitehead, writer for *Southwest Brewing News*, described it as "well-balanced with a nutty maltiness and a slightly bitter crisp finish. The ESB is brewed with a blend of West Coast hops giving it a subtle grapefruit note and an American character." It sure caught fire, as it won the gold medal over fifty-six entries at the 2014 World Beer Cup in the ESB category. He did not dabble much with adjuncts until he brewed the Los Naranjos coffee stout with locally roasted coffee from Elemental Roasters in Oklahoma City. A doppelbock and double ESB were brewed in special-release bombers to take advantage of the big, boozy beer trends that were taking over the craft beer community. Brewing in Missouri led to new points of distribution, as Kansas City was selected to be the first area of distribution outside of Oklahoma. "The energy and civic pride are similar to what we see happening in Oklahoma City right now with strong support for the arts and community in general," Stumph told *Feast* magazine. The contract brewing continued with O'Fallon until around late 2017, when Chris realized that the new alcohol law changes of 2016 were going to open brand-new opportunities for his dream to run a full-scale brewery.

The city of Norman was a bit underserved in his mind, so it seemed like a place that would appreciate a local business. With new endeavors came new changes. Brad and Chris parted ways, and Ole Marcussen, a retired civil engineer who hails from Norway, took the helm as his new business partner. Plans were drawn up, and the ten-thousand-square-foot building was filled with a thirty-barrel brewhouse and massive stainless steel fermenters to make about five thousand barrels of beer per year. "We knew with the laws changing the taproom had to be designed not only to be a full distribution brewery but a destination taproom. Distribution was always our lifeline and with the new facility we went straight to canning since we felt it was a better vessel over bottles," recalled Chris. Black Mesa went through a transformation with a new format of twelve-ounce cans, new beers like Big Wheel IPA and Cave Dweller Red Ale and the Kolsch updated to Mountain Boomer Kolsch in reference to the state lizard. The Los Naranjos recipe was adjusted a bit and is brewed seasonally. "It's been a long road, just doing all the contract brewing, not really having control of your brews. Then, we cut ground here in March of 2018, so this has been about a year-long process.... It feels really good now," Sanders told Mack Burke of the *Norman Transcript*.

Anthem Brewing Company (2013–Present)

Another brewery from the OKCity Brewing club, Anthem Brewing, was started by Matt Anthony. "I remember fondly back in 2000 my wife, then fiancée, bought me a Mr. Beer kit and I hadn't shown any interest whatsoever in brewing. So, I made a batch and I was taken aback and thought, hey this tasted pretty good, so I brewed on it a couple more times," Matt recalled. After a few years, Matt met up with a co-worker who was way more serious about the hobby with a full brew system in his garage. The itch started growing after another year or so brewing with his friend, and Matt bought his first homebrewing system from the Brew Shop in 2004. Immediately he was hooked, doing extract kits and really delving into British styles. Around early 2006, he dove into all-grain brewing with tips from the Brewing Network and joined the High Plains Draughters homebrew club. As fate would have it, he met Gary Shellman, who was selling his all-grain system, which Matt bought that night. In May 2006, Matt brewed his very first batch of beer on that kit, and he thought to himself, "This is definitely something I want to do for a living."

After settling into his craft for two to three years, he taught himself as much as he could and dialed in his recipes. In 2009, planning started for Anthem, which originally started as the Brothers Stout. The name was derived from two friends who wanted to create a brewpub with an Irish pub concept. He was still leaning heavily toward making British beers until he experienced Duchesse de Bourgogne, a Flanders red ale aged for eighteen months in wine barrels, and changed course to Belgian styles. Later that year, he flew out to Savor, a craft beer and food festival, where he met his heroes like Jim Koch of Boston Brewing and Sam Calagione of Dogfish Head; after he returned, he wrote up his business plan. Like a fine aged Duchesse, another year and a half went by, and in 2011, Matt ventured to the Craft Brewers Conference in San Francisco. Imagine a place where you can learn all you ever wanted about creating a brewery, securing ingredients, learning to market it and make money on swag—the CBC was the place to gain all of that. While there, he ran into Oklahoma brewers from Marshall Brewing and Krebs Brewing who gave him lots of support as the industry was ready to embrace more competition.

However, such a thing was a tall order, as the only real business plan was a full distribution brewery since a taproom model was not legally in place in Oklahoma. "At the time, I don't know if it was just being young or seeing the wave of breweries open across the country where everyone is the next big regional brewery and I wanted lots of people to try my beers so a taproom wasn't really a thought at that time." The dreams were grand, and by the end of 2011, Matt had formed his LLC and finished his business plan. However, he didn't have $500,000 to get it started. "With Anthem, my goal was to blend the things I love from the old world with the unrestricted passion for innovation of the new world. To make beers that are an expression of myself and what I love most, without regard for rigid style guides. Beers that are a tribute to individualism. These beers are my anthem to the world," Matt told Nick of the *Thirsty Beagle* beer blog. While looking for investors, Matt caught wind of the new OKCity Brewing venture opening up. Chase Healey, who had just left COOP to brew for Redbud Brewing, invited him to check out the brewery and be a part of a new incubator. This was the perfect answer to start up his company with a smaller investment. Around that time, the Kangs, who owned the co-op, brought in their friend Allen Musser, who was looking to invest in a local brewery and met with Matt in January 2012.

After a few meetings, Allen was hooked, and things started to move fast. On Matt's thirty-third birthday, he quit his day job of eleven years and started a new path with Anthem Brewing full time.

There was only one problem. "I had never brewed on a commercial system, obviously just being a homebrewer, and so the week before the first batch of my flagship beer Golden One I reached out to Chase to learn how to brew on the system. There wasn't a step-by-step breakdown, I just watched him brew and asked a few questions here and there." Matt's goal was to create a line of small-batch boutique beers and focus on sours and barrel aging and bottling. Unfortunately, the bottling machine never worked, so he pivoted back to creating some easy-drinking Belgian-style beers. Golden One was accepted really well at myriad local festivals throughout Oklahoma. "My next beer, Arjuna, I completely screwed up and had to dump. At the time Black Mesa moved in and capacity tightened up with three breweries and time constraints made me retract and focus on Golden One for the next six months." Eventually, Chase left Redbud to pursue his own microbrewery, and Mustang took over ownership of the co-op in January 2013.

"Around that point, Allen and I were discussing strategies. Fermenter space was slim so having three breweries in there all doing well showed there wasn't much room to grow," Matt recalled. With a desire to brew sour beers that require open fermentation and using lacto or pedio yeast strains, it would have been too risky to affect someone else's beer. Both agreed that it was time to fly the incubator nest, and they found a used fifteen-barrel system from a brewpub that closed down in Chicago. Then, on that fateful day in May 2013, the tornado struck the co-op and halted any production from Anthem for about six months. So, no beer was being made, but this allowed time for construction and installation of equipment at a new facility. "That led up to October of 2013 and all we were waiting for was our TTB license from the government. But right before we were able to get it, there was a government shutdown," recalled a humble Matt. It was a long winter wait, but not without its benefits, as Matt hired Will Perry as his first employee. Will had volunteered to brew at the co-op, and after working alongside him, Matt instinctively knew that this young go-getter was going places. During all this lag time and with the ABLE commission holding them back with paperwork, they started a barrel program of around sixty barrels of unique beers like Babylon and Pappy Burleson. By April, Arjuna, a wit beer, and Uroboros, an 8.5 percent Belgian stout aged on oak spirals, were released for keg sales. The Oklahoma Craft Brewers Festival was on the horizon in May, and Matt wanted to come out big. "The operators told us to have some fun with this and brew as many beers as you want, so we made like 20 beers and it was a lot of fun. The other highlight of that year was the brewmaster from Unibroue was doing a promotional tour through the U.S., and he stopped by Anthem. That was big for me being such a huge fan of Belgian beers and one of my favorite breweries. The compliment of my life was he told me this was one of the cleanest breweries he'd ever been in. That's better than telling a brewer I love your beer," recalled Matt happily.

Canning was the next step, so they found a used system up in Nebraska and brought it down to can their three beers. There was no looking back after that, as Anthem made a name for itself in the local drinking culture. "Seeing our cans on the shelf—that was the coolest thing in the world. That's what I feel like I've been working for. Having stuff out on draft was a really cool experience. But the goal was always to get stuff out to liquor stores and have a package that people could bring home. To finally see that—it's such a good feeling," Matt told Nick Trougakos of the *Oklahoman*. They were making a lot of beer with their "tank farm," with five open-top fermenters, six to eight fifteen-barrel unit tanks, then thirty-barrel tanks, then a bright tank, which led to a sixty-barrel bright tank along with a palletizer to the canning line to speed up production—all accumulated within three months. Around this point, the taproom tasting law was in place, and people could come and visit the brewery and taste a few samples. It was still frustrating to Matt that they could not sell on site. In November 2014, Matt was approached by the very people who helped get him started all those years ago. Some reps from Mr. Beer had a brewmaster series spotlighting brewers who started with its kit and went on to brew professionally. Matt formulated a recipe for his Golden One to send out to the Mr. Beer members.

Near the closing of 2014, Matt and his investors had come to a point of disagreement about brewing styles and how to move forward with the company that ultimately led to him part ways with Anthem in January 2015. Matt recounted in his exit interview with the *Oklahoman*, "Anthem was, and will always be my baby, birthed from my heart and mind years ago," he said. "The level of support I received from friends, family, and strangers over the past few years has been astounding. I got to see my dream made into a reality, and I will always be extremely grateful for this experience." Anthem's brewer, Will Perry, had moved on to Texas, and their newest recruit, Patrick Lively, came on to help with brewing from a previous role in production management. Patrick started like most beer lovers and started brewing at home for three to four years. When he learned of COOP Ale Works opening up in Oklahoma City, he and current brewmaster Blake Jarolim knocked on the door. "At first it was a lot of volunteer work that led to part- and full-time work in the brewery," said Patrick. He ended up becoming the production manager in 2010 until August 2014, when COOP moved into a larger facility that Patrick had left with intentions of starting his own venture. Around October of that year, he was approached by Allen Musser and came on to take over the brewer's role and help get their products in shape. "They were going through some growing pains like most small breweries do in scaling up and production planning and making sure you have beer in the tanks and product leaving as orders come in." Patrick agreed to come on in a temporary role and work alongside Matt. With Matt's departure, his role became a lot more prevalent as president and head brewer of Anthem in January 2015.

With only producing about eight hundred barrels of beer the year prior, it was clear to Patrick that the owner wanted to expand into a production-oriented brewery, and with his talents, he led them to almost quadruple growth in the next three years. Times were good, and they brewed up an IPA with a solid malt backbone to branch out past the initial Belgian-style beers being offered. A new era began when they left the original core and transitioned to more traditional American-style beers. Brewing for a brand that didn't resonate with the same brewing philosophy was a challenge and one that slowly worked itself away from Matt's original vision. Anthem still brews its original core Belgian-style beers along with hop-forward beers, all under a new branding that took place in 2019.

Roughtail Brewing Company (2012–Present)

Ever since he was in middle school, Blaine Stansel dreamed of being an entrepreneur. Armed with an undergraduate degree in management from the University of Oklahoma, he went into retail. "I loathed it," he told the *Oklahoman*. Not all dreams start out perfect, so he went back to school for an MBA in finance and again found the entrepreneur lifestyle calling him. "I took a course in entrepreneurship and I fell in love with it. I ended up doing a double concentration in finance and entrepreneurship." What really projected Stansel down the road was winning the 2008 Donald W. Reynolds Governor's Cup with a business plan focused on technology that reduced the number of injections diabetics took. He soon took a role with Charlesson LLC as its director of finance in Oklahoma City. Fate had other ideas:

During a trip to Munich in 2007, I developed a passion for craft beers. The quality and the culture around the beers is what intrigued me to start my home brewery. I was visiting Munich after a summer internship in Europe and absolutely fell in love with the culture surrounding the beer. Aventinus made by Schneider & Sons really made a large impact on me. I decided then that I wanted to make homebrew. For a couple of years I dabbled in homebrewing, mainly in the German style beers, but it wasn't until the Great American Beer Festival in 2010 that I decided I wanted to make a career out of brewing.

Blaine met with a likeminded homebrewer named Tony Tielli at the newly formed Red Earth Homebrewers Club. The two quickly became friends and had the same passions about opening up a brewery. "Without the Governor's Cup, I wouldn't have had the opportunity to develop the skills needed to write an effective business plan and probably wouldn't have the confidence needed to start a business." Tony had been brewing for about ten years, moving from a simple kit to a system that eventually took over his garage. His beers won several awards across the country.

Originally, they had the vision to start in the Dallas market, which was booming at the time. For the name, they wanted a rough-sounding animal and settled on a particular gecko found in Texas. "When people think of geckos they don't normally picture a tough critter, but I would say this gecko's the exception. The name really sold it, though, as it exemplifies our style and approach. We are rough compared to the mass-marketed light lagers, and we view ourselves as invasive to the brewing industrial complex." With that, the search was on for a place to build out their vision for aggressive beers. Being an Oklahoman native, Blaine felt the potential to shine in Oklahoma City would far surpass the exploding market in Dallas. They landed on an early 1930s brick building zoned as a storage warehouse built originally by the Santa Fe Railroad and filed for a liquor license on October 19, 2012. From the start, there were multiple problems, as it wasn't properly zoned for manufacturing. "There's been a lot of those cool historical buildings that are just sitting abandoned because it's literally more expensive to bring them up to code than it is to tear it down and build a new metal building," Blaine told the *Thirsty Beagle* blog. After six building plan drafts to bring it into compliance and a lot of wasted time, they were told they needed a fire suppression system for the entire building to the tune of more than six figures. "We received all of our equipment there on Christmas Eve 2012 at five in the morning, with a team of like 12

A Handcrafted History

Tony Tielli mashes in their first beer, Red Republic, in February 2013. *Courtesy of Roughtail Brewing Company.*

guys. We didn't have any equipment—we had a pallet jack and that was it. We didn't have a forklift—we had nothing. We were literally carrying the stuff off the truck by hand. It was crazy. We got it all moved into that building, and then we found out that building wasn't going to work, so we had to transport it all over here [to Midwest City]." By January 21, 2013, they had signed a lease on a new building that ticked all the boxes, and the city was working with them on the transition.

It was important to the two owners that they started with their own facility. Tony relayed their reasons to the *Thirsty Beagle* blog: "First, our goal is to provide perfection in a pint glass, every single time to every single customer… and we think it's vital to have direct control over the entire brewing process and production facility in order to make this a reality. Roughtail beer is about putting our local craft, our art, into kegs and cans…not paying someone else to do the hard work." The second reason was the fact that as a production brewery, they needed to brew a lot and keep quality consistency with confidence to produce beer for Oklahoma and eventually other regional areas. They wanted to have the freedom to brew one-off batches, seasonal and experimental brews. Incorporated in 2012, they started up production and had their first three "Aggressive. Flavor Forward." beers launched in March 2013 at Tapwerks in Oklahoma City. They released them in sixteen-ounce four-pack cans. The Republic Red, a hoppy red ale; 12th Round Strong Ale; and their flagship, Roughtail IPA, were brewed to be aggressive,

Blaine Stansel stands with their first shipment of kegs, which went to Capital Distributing on April 1, 2013. *Courtesy of Roughtail Brewing Company.*

palate-busting beers. "One of the goals in creating these specific beers is to push the boundaries of taste," Tony explained at their launch. The ten-barrel brewhouse was set up for distribution along with a small area up front for a potential taproom to serve samples. Roughtail was about brewing big, intense beers that Oklahoma had not seen yet from the other breweries. For IPA Day in July 2013, they released Hoptometrist, which weighed in at 10 percent ABV and over 100 IBUs (International Bitterness Units). The seasonal beer was quickly adopted into their year-round schedule. Their first stout was a one-off Russian imperial stout called Rock Tsar, released in a 750ml bottle; it featured big roasted malt and chocolate flavors. On April 5, 2014, they celebrated their first anniversary with a party at the brewery that featured a dozen beers to sample, and they released a double IPA in twenty-two-ounce bombers to the public.

After the sampling bill passed in 2013, they eventually jumped into the low-point brewing game with their Jaragua Pale Ale for sale on draft and to go in growlers in the summer of 2014. "We can make 3.2 beers really well," said Tony Tielli. "The main goal is to expand craft beer culture and bring some increased form of brewery awareness to Oklahoma and make great session beers that people will drink." That being said, Roughtail finally brewed its flagship IPA two years after opening. Quite unorthodox, but the team had secured the hops they wanted in a market of heavy demand and perfected their brewing method to produce the IPA they wanted to start with. "The new Roughtail IPA is brewed using a new strain of clean fermenting yeast that lets the hop flavor and aroma really shine, a neutral malt profile that provides just enough support for the hops and a heavy dose of Simcoe, Citra, Centennial, Summit and Columbus hops," said Tony.

To celebrate its third anniversary, Roughtail expanded distribution into Kansas through Worldwide Beverage of Lenexa in April 2016. One of its most iconic hop-forward beers to date debuted in a series called Adaptation, where the team made an experimental IPA each time. Later named Everything Rhymes with Orange, the beer was a draft-only release and became an instant success. It was packaged in four-packs a few months later in 2016 and continues to be one of its best-selling beers to date. One of the reasons it enjoyed success was experimenting with new hops; it had a contract through 2019 to guarantee that it wouldn't be affected by any hop shortages.

Roughtail kept the lights on with its distribution model, but it was tight not having a taproom to sell its high-point products. A local beer enthusiast, Kevin Hall, formulated a grass-roots movement with likeminded Oklahomans called the League of Oklahomans for Change in Alcohol Laws (LOCAL). The goal was to raise money for a lobbyist to work with legislators on changing the antiquated laws. "I would hire another person tomorrow," Tielli told the *OK Gazette*. "We've sold a ton of beer [to stores and bars], but we are barely keeping the lights on by doing that. It's that taproom business that allows small breweries like us to survive." As showcased thus far, changing the outdated alcohol laws proved difficult in coordinating enough consensus. Their motivation was steeped in the economic benefits that would increase the tourism and hospitality industry along with generous tax revenue brought into the state. "If there is going to be change, it's going to come from a group like [LOCAL]," Tielli said. "If brewery owners go and try to talk to lawmakers, they are going to look at that as us trying to advance our own businesses. But when lawmakers see that there are a ton of people who are taxpayers, voters and citizens in their state that support this, that is a much different situation for them." Tony's words were an insight into how the next few years would play out in the local beer scene and of things to come.

Prairie Artisan Ales (2012–Present)

With the success of several beers and brewing endeavors under his belt, Chase Healey left Redbud Brewing to pursue his own passion for crafting truly unique beers unaccustomed to the average drinking palate of most Oklahomans. The son of a schoolteacher and local newscaster, Chase thought he'd follow in his father's footsteps during his time at Oklahoma University. Like many other brewers who got their start, Chase homebrewed in college, and then a new opportunity opened for him. "I didn't even walk at my graduation because I was busy brewing," Chase told Michael Kiser of the podcast *Good Beer Hunting*. He eventually took the mindset of his dad that he'd support himself with his craft after brewing for COOP and Redbud and began making beer for himself. He took a brewmaster job in Texas for a small brewery that lasted six months. However, Chase was drawn to the lifestyle of a gypsy brewer, like famous European brewers Mikkeler and Evil Twin. So, he ventured back to Oklahoma and rented out space in Krebs to develop artisan beers, looking beyond doing the "safe, high-volume" brewing model. After a fateful lunch one day with Krebs owner Zach Prichard, Chase laid out his ideas, beers and marketing, and Zach agreed to give him some space at the brewery. "To me, the brewing industry has changed to where a brewer can go outside of the norm and still find an audience." He landed on the name Prairie due to the region Oklahoma was known for and his pride of growing up as an Okie. "Artisan Ales helps define the beers. They are complex, unfiltered, bottle-conditioned ales." Chase mentioned the concept to his younger brother, Colin, and wanted him to draw up a logo for the new brewery. It almost never happened, as Colin was swamped with homework at the time. "I decided to make this really silly drawing quickly and I left it on the kitchen counter for him to see when he woke up, and he really liked it." Two comedic prairie dogs never made it to any labels but marked the dry humor Chase was looking for. The act of kinship would later prove to be a successful career path for budding artist and trained musician Colin, who plays double bass for the Tulsa Signature Symphony. "I think Prairie has been an interesting thing because I have been able to develop as an artist in front of our whole market. Because when we started the brand, I did not have a specific idea what I wanted it to be. It has sort of evolved in front of everyone," Colin told the *Tulsa World*.

At the time, Chase took on a small brewing job in Dallas, planning his next moves while driving back and forth to Krebs. "The Prichards are just

Prairie Ale label. *Courtesy of Prairie Artisan Ales.*

awesome people. They let me sleep in their guest bedroom three days a week, and we got the project off the ground." Chase had a mission to set a trend of brewing specialty "one-off" beers that had not been done often in 2013. The pairing between the two artists worked out well, and it helped to have a well-established high-end beer importer like Shelton Brothers drum up international interest for them. Chase had garnered interest from the Massachusetts-based distributor in his early brewing days when he poured at festivals. "The timing seemed to work out," Chase said. "I've wanted to work with Shelton for years as I am very inspired by their portfolio." His first beer, Prairie Ale, debuted at the First Draft beer festival, put on by the Tulsa Press Club. Chase poured his beer from twenty-two-ounce cork and caged bottles to emphasize the unique flagship beer. The label featured a light bulb and garland from a failed oil painting Colin had attempted. "Our goal from the beginning has been to create a company that connects with people all over the world, not just our local market," said Chase. Demand grew after he sent fifteen barrels to Shelton Brothers and then thirty barrels of his beer Prairie Hop and Prairie Standard. "I'd seen the success that Jolly Pumpkin and Saint Somewhere had had working through the Shelton Brothers to sell small amounts of beer throughout the country, and they were willing to take our brand on," Healey told *Craft Beer & Brewing* magazine. "That helped us to get our beer into a lot of places pretty quickly and gain some early recognition."

Within nine months, they were pumping out fifteen beers, with a majority of the production out of Krebs. In the summer of 2013, they developed a brewhouse at Forty-Ninth West Avenue in west Tulsa near Chandler Park, where initially they wanted to install a disc golf course. The small industrial area came with a large gravel parking lot that would become a destination point for thousands of beer fanatics. The ten-barrel brewhouse held several fermenters that were funded by a Kickstarter fundraiser, cold storage and offices. Loads of various oak barrels from Portugal and France lined the walls for aging beer. Chase brought over his love for wild ales from his time experimenting at Redbud and captured live yeast cultures that surrounded the brewery. "Things tend to come together a bit more organically. It's much less structured, for better or worse, but that's how my mind operates."

Above: Guests tour the brewery and barrel room of Prairie Artisan Ales, while owner Chase Healey pours samples, February 22, 2014. *Photo by the author.*

Opposite: A typical bottling day at American Solera in Tulsa, Oklahoma. *Photo by the author.*

His first beer brewed out of the Tulsa location was a farmhouse ale saison named Potlatch, a collaborative beer with Omnipollo of Sweden that was deemed a funky, fruity beer due to the types of yeast used. Conveniently enough, Prairie opened its taproom doors when the new HB 1341 law was passed to allow beer tasting at the site of the brewery. He continued to create up to fourteen more beers, leading up to Prairie's first tour on December 21, 2013, including the Potlatch; Elizabeth, a farmhouse ale brewed for their sister; and Legend, an 11 percent golden Belgian-style ale. Several braved the crazy weather to learn about the brewing process and this diamond-in-the-rough brewery in humble Oklahoma. Chase quickly fulfilled his dream of meeting and working with those brewers he admired after only a year into his endeavor. The Healey brothers' passport books filled quickly with trips to Europe, where they brewed at De Proef and poured at festivals in Amsterdam. Through his travels, Chase was inspired to create a new, larger facility called Prairie Farms, which was staged for

A Handcrafted History

buildout in Glenpool, Oklahoma. The large 3,500-square-foot ranch-style brewery would have a large production site, with plans to add another 4,000-square-foot building on the seventeen-acre lot. Unfortunately, after all their presentations to the city, a discrepancy about the sewage system halted all further plans and the idea was scrapped.

Then, in January 2014, the Bomb! dropped. What is considered to this day an iconic and now year-round beer set the tone for the types of beers Prairie would go on to make, especially in the high-alcohol, adjunct stouts category. Bomb! delivered immense flavors thanks to ingredients of cacao nibs, vanilla beans, ancho chiles and locally roasted coffee beans from Nordaggios of Tulsa. This small-batch 13 percent imperial stout was released with a blue glittery wax encapsulating a twelve-ounce bottle and quickly snatched up by local consumers. Brewed at Choc Brewing, cases of Bomb! were sold out in mere hours at liquor stores around Oklahoma, and it was named one of RateBeer's Top 100 Beer in the World for three consecutive years. The brewery produced around seven thousand barrels of beer in 2016, pushing the limits Chase ever imagined for this small-scale brewery, with accolades again from RateBeer for top 100 Brewery in the World out of more than twenty-two thousand breweries for several years in a row. Prairie was always intended to be a brewery that experimented with techniques, hardly ever duplicating the same beer and lacking a core lineup like most breweries did. Chase soon found himself split between the large-scale production in Krebs and trying to focus on the small-scale artisan beers in the new Tulsa facility—certainly a method that took more risks and pushed the boundaries of what people in Oklahoma have previously imbibed. It was daring at the time to create something people may not like, but this eventually brought out likeminded consumers who wanted to experience craft beer that was brewed in other states but had no access to them. As Chase was tasked with more than he could handle, his wife, Erica Healey, soon joined the family business in a part-time role. "I was working full time as a therapist in town and left that job and just kind of dove right in to see what I could do to help and have been here ever since." Erica held down the day-to-day operations while Chase focused on the beers.

As production increased, there came a serious time when Chase had to step back and consider if the brewery still met his original goals. With Krebs producing almost all of Prairie's beers, Chase made the tough but professional decision to sell the rights to all of Prairie's beers to Krebs Brewing Company. From a press statement issued by Krebs president Zach Prichard, he said:

> *Early on, I had been interested in actually owning a part of Prairie. Since I already felt like the beers were a partnership it only made sense. Last year that opportunity presented itself. Chase agreed to allow Krebs Brewing*

A Handcrafted History

Assistant Brewer Jake Miller (left), and Sales and Marketing Director Wes Morrison clean out the bottle filler before filling bottles with a new Prairie beer. Photo by the author.

Company to acquire the Prairie brands. It is a humbling move that shows Chase continues to trust us to innovate, make great beer, and share Prairie across the globe. I do not take that trust lightly.

Between Chase's ambitious goals and the hardworking crew at Krebs, Prairie was certainly a collaborative effort between both companies. The inevitable merger led to new endeavors, like the Prairie Brewpub set up in the Brady Arts District in Tulsa. The current liquor laws kept them from actually brewing beer until much later, but the spot was a destination point for international fans to sample local food and Prairie beers with several guest taps. Chase held a kind of ambassadorial role after the sale but quickly developed his next venture. American Solera was founded in 2016 and has quickly become highly desired with the fruited sours, barrel-aged adjunct stouts and hazy IPAs.

Oklahoma Beer

Dead Armadillo Brewing (2013–Present)

Why did the chicken cross the road? To show the armadillo it was possible. This is just one of many armadillo jokes that founder Tony Peck continues to hear from customers. Originally an animal that was native to the Deep South, armadillos have migrated north and can be spotted dead all across the major highways and turnpikes of Oklahoma. One particular dead varmint was found in a shed while Tony was cleaning up his parents' property in Kansas, where he hails from. At the time, he was looking for the perfect name for his brewery he was starting and pitched the silly name of Dead Armadillo to his partners. What was supposed to be a joke actually stuck, and thus Dead Armadillo Brewing Company was born a few months later. But let's back up a minute to where this eclectic brewery originated.

Founding member Mason Beecroft, originally from Oregon, was a Lutheran pastor for eleven years, having studied historical theology at Dallas Theological Seminary. After moving to Tulsa, he converted to Catholicism to focus more on his homebrewing hobby, which was strictly prohibited in the Lutheran faith. He had enjoyed brewing and perfected his craft for some fifteen years when he met with co-founder Tony Peck at one of his services at Grace Lutheran Church in Tulsa. Tony, an IT professional for fifteen years, learned the art of brewing in 2006 at a summer vacation Bible school that Mason called "Christian Art of Brewing Beer," where he and the parents would sit and drink homebrew while the kids had their lessons. "The parents would drop the kids off, and all the parents would come out to the back patio, and we'd sit back there and drink beer," said Beecroft of his lessons. Tony's co-worker, Chris "The Hulk" Barba, also had the brewing bug for some seven years when he was brought into the conversation, and the holy trinity of owners was now complete. All of them had come to a point in their lives that they loathed their normal day jobs and took the plunge into opening a brewery. With nearly thirty years of brewing practice between them, they started to seriously discuss opening up a brewery in downtown Tulsa. Only one preceded them (Marshall Brewing), so they knew the market was hungry for more local craft beer. They perfected their craft in Tony's garage on nights and weekends, combining their interests for highly drinkable beers to match the local market. They incorporated in 2012, and the crew tested out their recipes (their signature American Amber Ale, a wheat; their Nine Band IPA, which used nine different hops during the ninety-minute boil; and the Black Hop IPA) at local beer festivals like Wild Brew, McNellie's

Dead Armadillo Brewing's brewhouse. *Photo by the author.*

Harvest Beer Festival, Tulsa First Draft and the Hop Jam to gain feedback and raise awareness of the new brewery.

In 2012, a Kickstarter campaign was launched to "Raise the Dead" and fund a canning line and cans for the guys to distribute out to the state. In the video, there was a building they referenced as their new home. Unfortunately, that location, among others, fell through as the process of looking for a home turned out to be the most difficult task. "Craft brewers we talked to told us you want people who care about the industry—people who love beer," said marketing director Chris Barba. Buildings around Tulsa were not properly zoned for such a brewery, and the industry was so niche that many city departments did not know how to regulate them. Typically, finding investors and raising capital was the hardest part of opening a brewery; however, they were fortunate to find some who understood their vision and didn't demand a high percentage of ownership. So they raised money by selling merchandise because they could not sell beer yet. They continued to hit the festival circuit around the state for the next year and a half but lost Chris along the journey. The flagship Amber Ale was eventually mass-produced into cans by 2013. The copper-colored 6.3 percent ABV beer was described by Tony Peck as "eminently drinkable and well-balanced with notes of caramel sweetness; roasted crystal malt and a slightly bitter finish from the late addition Columbus and Cascade hops. The head on the beer is slightly off-white and laces down the glass throughout the drinking experience."

By the summer of 2013, they had multiple craft enthusiast accounts pouring their Amber on draft, like McNellie's, R Bar and Tapwerks. By the spring of 2014, they had become overwhelmed by the demand. "We are at capacity, and Roughtail is at capacity, so it's almost like we are in the way at this point," Peck said. "We're on close to 50 tap handles in restaurants and bars in the state, but we haven't been out selling in two to three months. We can't meet additional production." With the boys maxing out space at Roughtail and only able to brew three times a month, they were desperate to find a home for themselves. They had been working with McGraw Realty and agent Neil Dailey, who chauffeured them around numerous buildings that would meet all of their needs. "He went above and beyond to research exactly what a brewery would need in Tulsa," said Tony. As happenstance would have it, Neil was on the board of the Tulsa Youth Services and at a meeting had mentioned that he was looking for an industrial building in which a brewery could set itself up. Another member referred him to the owner of Fourth Street Auto, a board member as well, which was located across the street. The rest was fate, and seven months later, they moved into the seven-thousand-square-foot building at 1004 East Fourth Street in the Pearl District of Tulsa. "It was actually one of the cleanest places we had found. It had recently been revamped with new tile and an updated front room that is perfect for our taproom," said Tony. After searching for two years, they hit the jackpot with a location shadowed by downtown Tulsa, with a bike trail and walking distance to Tulsa's nightlife.

They created approachable beers that connected with the community, like the Hooligan Ale, an English-style bitter, for the Tulsa Athletic Soccer Club. Despite the consistent roadblocks, they continued to be surprised by local demand for their beer. "The industry is moving toward local and regional breweries," Beecroft told the *Tulsa World*. "Craft beer fans are not loyal to a brand like a Bud man or Miller man. They want to try everything that's out there, and that's cool. If laws were different, we would have a lot more craft brewers in Oklahoma right now." Regardless of their short tenure at Roughtail, they gained a wealth of knowledge and went on to commission the same brewing system from China in November 2014. The hardest part was communicating with the manufacturers and waiting the full year for buildout, shipment and customs bureaucracy. If that wasn't difficult enough, the worst hurdle was waiting on city permits due to their niche industry. "There was definitely a learning curve for the city as they tried to determine what we needed to be zoned as a Heavy Industrial license from a Commercial Light that our building was originally set as," said Mason. It was an arduous process that took a lot of money, time and mounds of paperwork. "We received a lot of restaurant criteria because the Health Department didn't know how to regulate us. Luckily, Marshall went through a lot of those headaches, and we were able to bypass unnecessary updates to the space which saved us a lot of money," said Tony. Demand continued for the sweet nectar of Amber, as all of the kegs were pre-sold as soon as they were picked up and they could never keep up with canned beer.

In 2015, they were approached by the Hanson brothers to collaborate on a beer for the Tulsa market. "Really the collaboration started with saying, 'How can we start brewing with these guys? How can we bring in some more beer?'" said Taylor Hanson. It was a way for all of them to show their love for Tulsa and brew a beer together. In a short time, they hashed out a recipe for the robust Inland Porter, named after the Port of Catoosa, the most inland port in the United States. "I have a special affection for porters; it was the first beer that turned me on to craft beer," Beecroft said. "It's an American version of a traditional English session beer that comes in at 6.5 percent ABV. I think it hit the mark for being a nice seasonable porter."

The beer was released in March 2016 on draft at Fassler Hall in Tulsa and liquor stores in twenty-two-ounce bombers. Hanson would transition to cans and contract-brewed their Mmmhops and spiced farmhouse saison at Dead Armadillo for distribution.

The new brewhouse had its kinks, but they maxed it out with seventy barrels of fermentation space, and by 2016 they had brewed about one thousand barrels of beer for distribution. "If we didn't have those constantly full, there was a major problem," said Tony. The front taproom held a six-tap cooler for the possibility of serving high-point beer if the rumored legislation allowing breweries to serve on site ever came to fruition. They had several 3.2 ABV beers available to go but held strong on brewing for distribution to local markets to increase revenue. Overall, the idea of them opening up was predicated on brewing Amber Ale, but they were encouraged that their passion had paid off. They put out a product people loved just as much as they did. Another opportunity to expand recognition came in a few marketing efforts in the city of Tulsa. "One of our investors has several connections with the Tulsa Drillers and always wanted to do special events with us at the stadium. What we came up with was a branded beer kiosk with a large cooler for can sales along with all four of our year-round beers on draft, including a new Low & Outside session pale ale brewed with oats that will also be available in 12 oz. cans. We used some pretty low alpha hops but still got them in there to make a pale ale and used oats to bump up mouthfeel and body."

Then, in the fall of 2017, Tulsa saw its first brewery-themed bar at Tulsa International Airport (TIA). Construction began on May 1, 2017, to revamp the entire food and beverage offerings due to the end of a contract from the previous management group. After a presentation and showing TIA its marketing, Dead Armadillo was approached as finalists and voted in after about nine months of deliberation. "We're Phase 1, luckily, so the sports bar in terminal A will be boarded up and gutted with a timetable of 90 days which will put us around August 1st and the Dead Armadillo Tarmac Taproom and Restaurant should be opening up at the airport." It mimics the look of the original taproom on Fourth and Madison. "We have put a lot of work into it. This is a homebrewer's dream," Peck said. "We love craft beer, and I love the brewing process. It is amazing how far we have come from what started as just a hobby. I was just intending to brew my own beer. Now, I love sharing it with people."

A Handcrafted History

Elk Valley Brewing (2013–Present)

My beer philosophy is simple: I brew beer that I love to drink and I believe you will too.

—*John Elkins, founder of Elk Valley*

Ever since his first sip of Raspberry Porter from Breckenridge Brewing out of Colorado in the mid-'90s, John Elkins changed his outlook on what beer could be. Living in Denver with his best friend and future best man Dave, they moved back to Oklahoma in 1999 and eventually got into homebrewing. "At the time there really wasn't the internet like we have today so you had to go to local brew shops, pick their brains and peruse countless books to gain the secrets of brewing good beer." When they both went to the Great American Beer Festival in Denver a few years later, that vibe and energy followed them home, and they were determined to create a brewery one day. After a while, the former roommates grew apart, and the dream lingered as a hobby while John enjoyed a career at Tinker Air Base as a B-52 mechanic. He would attend monthly meetings with the High Plains Draughters and perfect his craft while enjoying the ability to perfect his homebrew recipes.

While John became more serious about brewing, retrofitting his garage into a nanobrewery, he learned that his best friend had passed away. John was now determined to keep their passion for good beer alive and started to look into making his dream a reality. Around early 2012, he accumulated a bit of equipment along with several investors and located a space to start his brewery. However, at the zero hour, just nine days before closing on his building, John was in the parking lot of Roughtail about to inspect its canning line, which he planned on purchasing. "I was in the car on a conference call with my investors and they came to me with several major operational changes that quite frankly I wasn't about to make. I told them sorry and I had to walk away from the deal. At the time it was painful but I knew I would not be happy." Deflated after he came so close to his dream, John stepped away from brewing in October 2013. As his next step weighed on him, he decided to incorporate his company and formed an LLC in November 2013 for tax purposes and because of all of the overhead he had in his garage. Elk Valley Brewing Company was now official. The name stemmed from a childhood nickname since the seventh grade, "Elk," because his last name is Elkins. "I figured, we're starting from the ground up so where do you start? You don't start at the top of the mountain; you start in the valley."

Initially, John negotiated with Battered Boar to brew on its system, but after crunching the numbers he realized that it couldn't logistically make it happen. John ended up taking the contract brewing route and signed a deal with Krebs Brewing that lasted about eight months. While Krebs had the space, John had to haul three large thirty-barrel fermenters to Krebs in order to store his beer. He brought to market beers like his pale ale, Nemesis Coffee Stout and Experimental IPA. His beer was received well initially and helped him gain the confidence to continue brewing and build capital for a permanent location. While Oklahoma was his home, it wasn't the only location he scouted. John looked at potentially moving back to Colorado and even looked at spaces in Kansas and Arkansas. Ultimately, he decided to stay in Oklahoma, where he knew he'd have a tremendous amount of support behind him. In 2015, he inked a deal with Mustang Brewing to share space and half the production costs. This gave him an area with more room to work and also a taproom to increase his revenue. "I recall looking at the numbers and 90 kegs I sold into distribution had equaled the same revenue as 25 kegs in the taproom." To keep up with demand, he had

John Elkins at his last beer release before moving out of Mustang Brewing's old location. *Photo by the author.*

help from fellow homebrewer Will Perry, who was heavily involved with the evolving craft beer scene. Will eventually moved out to Colorado to gain more experience at places like Trinity Brewing and Colorado Brewing for several years.

John encountered another major blow when Mustang went out of business in 2017. He needed a place to brew, but there were not many other facilities that could handle his production. Through a stroke of luck, a new development was taking place in midtown Oklahoma City and proved to be the perfect forever home for his brewery. Complete with a rooftop deck, the new building provided a perfect space for his barrel aging and canning line to show off his new branding. With a dynamic marketing team behind John, Elk Valley has made a name for itself with a full lineup of approachable and big barrel-aged ales. "I love tinkering and experimenting with 7 to 15 barrel batches and if it doesn't turn out, on to the next. It's a gamble I'm willing to take," said John. He truly stands behind his product and actually listed his personal phone number on the packaging and website, taking calls daily regarding where you can find his beer. Now armed with a sales team, John spends more time brewing and developing the next beer he wants to drink.

THE OKLAHOMA BEER BOOM OF 2016

In October 2013, Anheuser-Busch's regional vice-president, Keith Diggs, said in a statement that "select additional Anheuser-Busch products with greater than 3.2 percent ABW will be made available in Oklahoma in response to consumer demand." This ended a thirty-six-year moratorium on the sale of full-strength Budweiser products in the state. Products like Budweiser, Black Crown and Lime-A-Ritas were soon brought in, as many questioned if this was the start of AB-InBev giving up control on quality and wanting to cash in on some 650 liquor stores at the time. "When a mega-multinational company makes a calculated move to gain market share in an otherwise flyover state, it signals a change in the culture of beer," said Wes Alexander of Marshall Brewing Company, referring to the recent growth of the local craft beer market. "While American light lager is still the king of the grocery and convenience store, that is not the case in restaurants, bars and liquor stores." With four more Oklahoma breweries coming online in 2015, there certainly was a change in consumer behavior and demand. Two of these new locations were Bedlam rivals of Norman and Stillwater, home to the state's top two universities, while the other two were near the Texas border near Beaver Bend State Park.

Just like the Sooner boomers to this state, there was a change in the air that signaled opportunity for those in the alcohol industry of Oklahoma. A general consensus among all these businesses agreed that change was needed, and this was the golden moment to do so. There were several major advocacy groups as well that played vital roles in educating the public on the benefits to the general consumer. The stage was set in January 2015, when two major bills were introduced in the Oklahoma State Senate, and the battle for alcohol reform began. SB 383, authored by freshman senator Stephanie Bice of Edmond, initially proposed amending Oklahoma law to allow for cold beer to be sold in liquor stores; however, it eventually became the legislative vehicle that would eliminate 3.2 beer in Oklahoma. Tulsa senator Brian Crain's SB 424 would amend state statutes to allow breweries to sell full-strength beer for both off-premises and on-premise consumption—a similar right that Oklahoma wineries had enjoyed since 1994. The following is a synopsis of the major players who created a shift in the way Oklahoma interpreted alcohol laws for the past sixty years.

Super Marshall Brothers

When we last discussed the Marshall brothers, they had just wrapped up the Tulsa Chamber's 2015 One Voice Day at the capitol in Oklahoma City. On their way out, friend Mike Thornbrugh, vice-president of government affairs for the QuikTrip Corporation, invited them to a meeting with Senator Clark Jolley, who at the time was in charge of budget appropriations, and newcomer Senator Stephanie Bice, who had just introduced SB 383. They arrived at a small conference room of a who's who of the Oklahoma alcohol industry from beer distributors, wholesalers and heavy industry leaders like Budweiser, Miller and Coors. "Walmart, Reasors, the Petroleum Marketers Association, which is the c-store lobby. We got the Grocers Association, Retail Liquor Association and we're these two craft brewers just kind of sitting over in the corner," said Adam Marshall. Senator Jolley basically introduced Senator Bice and her stance on the outdated alcohol laws, backed by polling done by one of the lobbyists from Walmart. "So what happens is [Senator] Jolley goes around, you know, if this is good, this polling of the people, they want to see this so we can either all get together and try to do this now and do a slow burn on this and phase it in over a couple of years because we're gonna rewrite sixty years of alcohol laws," recalled Adam. So with this grand meeting of the minds, Senator Jolley goes around the room and asks everyone to name what big change their industry wants to see. Confliction of general interests was inevitable and not all requests would be granted, but if enough spoke up and compromised, they could move rather swiftly to change the laws to benefit not only themselves but the consumer as well.

"One thing that we fought for with the law change was to be family-friendly, so parents can bring kids into the taproom," Marshall said. "We want to be a community gathering space where people can come and responsibly enjoy a beer and play some games with their kids." Eric's vision was to combine the old world and the new world with his craft but also incorporate a communal space where friends and family can meet. Local breweries had started discussions of banding together to be on the ground floor and have a lobbyist to keep their interests in check. "The Craft Brewers Association of Oklahoma Inc. (CBAO) is a 501(c)(6) trade association dedicated to educate and create awareness among legislators, regulators and the public of the issues facing the craft brewing industry in Oklahoma and to promote a healthy economic environment in Oklahoma that enables public choices in the marketplace for the consumer and opportunity and access to the marketplace by Oklahoma breweries." Made up of craft beer industry professionals, the group was formed in August 2015 to help educate the public of the new alcohol legislature through special events and fundraisers to hire a lobbyist.

District 22 State Senator Stephanie Bice

"The reason I did that is, over the years, so much legislation had been passed and added on to existing statute piecemeal," said Senator Stephanie Bice. "I wanted to reorganize it in a way that was easier to read and easier to find. It makes more sense to restructure and consolidate definitions." A freshman in the Oklahoma Congress, Senator Bice dove in with a hefty piece of legislation backed by fellow Republican colleagues that agreed there needed to be a change. Lobbyists for major retailers were also in talks at the time to shift toward a revised system, and the 2016 presidential election was the opportune moment to amend the constitution. "The idea of SB 383 was born from the craft brewing community that has blossomed over the past 5 years and the craft beer drinkers that find it frustrating you can't go to the store and buy a cold beer and take it and drink in the comfort of your own home," said Bice in an interview with the author. "My go-to beer is Hoegaarden. I would love to be able to go buy a six-pack of Hoegaarden to take home and enjoy one with dinner," she added on what she would drink once the bill passed.

The overarching goal was to eliminate the two-strength system for beer and allow regular strength to be sold in liquor, grocery and convenience stores along with wine. The plan of action was to hold a vote in the 2016

A Handcrafted History

State Senator Stephanie Bice speaks about the upcoming legislative session during the 2016 Oklahoma Craft Beer Summit at the Oak and Ore bar in Oklahoma City. *Photo by Tom Gilbert/*Tulsa World.

legislative session. There would be two different votes that would occur. One of them was to put a ballot initiative together to repeal Article 28 of the constitution. The second was to rewrite the laws the way they want to see them today. Access to minors being limited was at the forefront of their minds, so liquor was never an option to be sold in grocery or convenience stores. Oklahoma would be seen as a pioneer in repealing the two-strength system as at the time Kansas, Utah, Colorado and Minnesota were all still utilizing the same method. Advocates for the change stressed the importance of cold beer on shelves to maintain the integrity and increase the lifespan of the product, as well as the allure for more national craft brands to be sold in the state. Senator Jolley and Senator Bice made the argument: "Competition has always formed the basis of America's economy, and the more we can do to create a level playing field, the better. For example, rather than making beer runs across the state border, Oklahomans will now be able to keep their dollars at home. We believe updating Prohibition-era laws will also make it easier for employers to attract and retain a younger and more diversified workforce."

Oklahoma Beer

Free the Taps

According to a 2015 statistic by the Brewers Association, Oklahoma's craft beer industry was ranked 50th in the nation in the number of breweries per capita but ranked 33rd in economic impact at $416 million.
—*Tom Gilbert,* Tulsa World

"More than anything, today was a small step towards modernizing our laws. It also shows the power of grass-roots efforts," said Kevin Douglas Hall, president of League of Oklahomans for Change in Alcohol Laws, regarding SB383 and SB424 being passed through a special committee. "I head up a 501(c)(6) organization, LOCAL, dedicated to changing Oklahoma's liquor laws. We are an all-volunteer group of consumers dedicated to advocating for consumer rights. We consider ourselves the fifth-tier in Oklahoma's four-tier system, and as consumers fund the other tiers, we deserve a say in how we buy craft beer in the state," he relayed to the *Tulsa World*. Behind actions like emailing and phoning legislators about these new bills, LOCAL led prolific campaigns to educate and inspire actual consumers to contact their local legislators to pass these bills. "Yesterday we organized a direct action campaign to get consumers to call committee members and urge them to vote yes on both SB383 and SB424. What we learned today is that this campaign was very effective. One senator mentioned that the calls helped to sway her vote. What this tells me is that consumers have considerable power. We will keep the pressure up until both bills bear the governor's signature. Our work won't end with the passage of these bills," he told Tom Gilbert of the *Tulsa World*. "We look forward to advocating for and protecting consumer rights in Oklahoma for some time to come." Their efforts didn't go unnoticed, as on April 7, 2015, National Beer Day of all days, both bills passed through the Alcohol, Tobacco and Controlled Substances Committee by a vote of ten to zero and eventually went up for a vote in the House. "Today's vote on 424 was really about three things: fairness, jobs and consumer choice. It gave breweries the same rights as wineries. It created an industry overnight—beer tourism. And it gave the consumer what they wanted. A great day for Oklahoma," stated Kevin.

SB424 passed the Senate by a hefty vote of thirty-seven to four on March 9, 2015. In just over a month and a half, it passed the House by a large majority of sixty-six to nineteen on April 15, 2015. On May 24, 2016, both bills passed the state senate. "Today, a major hurdle was cleared on the Oklahoma Senate Floor as both SB 424 and SJR 68 were passed. Craft brewers and craft beer drinkers are one step closer to a progressive policy, which will allow the industry to grow. I congratulate the Craft Brewers Association, Sens. Crain and Jolley, and all the loyal craft beer fans who have worked hard to further our industry," said Wes Alexander. The act read as follows:

> *An Act relating to intoxicating liquors; amending 37 O.S. 2011, Section 521, as last amended by Section 17 of Enrolled House Bill No. 3201 of the 2nd Session of the 55th Oklahoma Legislature, which relates to acts authorized by licensees; allowing sale of beer to consumer on premises of brewery; and modifying language.*

The bill was finally enacted on August 24, 2016, ninety days after it was approved, to the joy of thousands of craft beer drinkers in Oklahoma. Most established breweries celebrated with special releases to mark the occasion. The pro-business movement opened the door for those looking to open a brewery to have access to capital faster than the "go big or go home" method that most people could not afford. "I would say that the law change really had an integral effect on the growth of craft beer in the state almost immediately," said Derek Duty, director of sales and marketing for Anthem Brewing Company. "You really saw the public interest start to elevate, as folks were getting around to see and learn more about the breweries and brewers in town, what they offered, and to offer up more support." The Oklahoma City metro area saw the number of breweries almost double after the act passed, as many were just waiting for its approval. "On the weekends, we're seeing a lot of visitors who come down to brewery hop," Eric Marshall said. "It's definitely added something to Tulsa that wasn't there before. I think people are really embracing it."

The Fight for Modernized Alcohol Laws

Senate Joint Resolution (SJR) 68 was altered as it moved through the state legislature and would eventually evolve into State Question 792. In order to amend the constitution, a vote of the people was needed. While many were on board with changes, there was opposition. Tensions mounted when Anheuser-Busch left the Beer Distributors of Oklahoma in February 2016 because of the language written in the bill in regards to distribution: "There shall be prohibited any common ownership between the manufacturing, wholesaling and retailing tiers, unless otherwise permitted by this subsection. A brewery may, following adoption of this Article, maintain or obtain licenses to distribute beer to no more than two (2) territories within the state, also known as brewery-owned branches." Overall, the company was concerned that the new measure would threaten hundreds of jobs if it had to sell off its distributorships. While it was for modernization of alcohol laws, it felt that with its historical contributions to the state and monetary impact, the measure should reflect that as well. In defense, Brett Robinson, president of the Beer Distributors of Oklahoma, rebutted this act with this statement:

> *The independent members of the Beer Distributors of Oklahoma fully support SJR 68 and commend Senator Clark Jolley, Senator Brian Bingman and Senator Stephanie Bice for their leadership on this complex issue. Because of their efforts Oklahomans could have the opportunity to vote this November to modernize Oklahoma's adult beverage laws in a fair, safe and responsible manner. Doing so will protect the independent three-tier system, provide more consumer choice, allow Oklahoma craft brewers to expand their markets and safeguard against foreign-owned brewery monopolies. Modernizing Oklahoma's alcohol laws is a complicated process, and many stakeholders, including BDO, have participated in the process. SJR 68 is the result of that process and is a quality piece of legislation.*

State Question 792 put to a vote of the people the repeal of Article 28 of the Oklahoma Constitution (Alcoholic Beverage Laws and Enforcement) and the enactment of Article 28A, as outlined in Senate Bill 383. The ballot language read as stated:

> *This measure repeals Article 28 of the Oklahoma Constitution and restructures the laws governing alcoholic beverages through a new Article 28A and other laws the Legislature will create if the measure passes. The new Article 28A provides that with exceptions, a person or company can have an ownership interest in only one area of the alcoholic beverage business-manufacturing, wholesaling, or retailing. Some restrictions apply to the sales of manufacturers, brewers, winemakers, and wholesalers. Subject to limitations, the Legislature may authorize direct shipments to consumers of wine. Retail locations like grocery stores may sell wine and beer. Liquor stores may sell products other than alcoholic beverages in limited amounts.*

A Handcrafted History

The Legislature must create licenses for retail locations, liquor stores, and places serving alcoholic beverages and may create other licenses. Certain licensees must meet residency requirements. Felons cannot be licensees. The Legislature must designate days and hours when alcoholic beverages may be sold and may impose taxes on sales. Municipalities may levy an occupation tax. If authorized, a state lodge may sell individual alcoholic beverages for on-premises consumption but no other state involvement in the alcoholic beverage business is allowed. With one exception, the measure will take effect October 1, 2018.

For consumers, this was a welcomed change that most wanted to see as a matter of convenience in accordance to their purchasing habits and was modeled after surrounding states like Arkansas, Kansas and Missouri. However, there was heavy opposition from the Retail Liquor Association of Oklahoma, so much so that it wrote a petition to strike down the state question, citing that it violated the Fourteenth Amendment of the U.S. Constitution. "State Question 792...creates an unfair marketplace for retail package stores by giving a series of advantages to other stores to sell as much beer and wine as they like without any of the restrictions placed on package stores," said RLAO president Bryan Kerr. It made a credible case in the matter of multiple licenses issued to major retailers, being limited to only 20 percent of non-alcohol product sales, and unable to allow children inside. Trying to rewrite sixty years of laws meant that not every party involved would get everything it wanted. The landscape and consumer behavior had changed drastically since 1959, and liquor stores that had been around since then would need to adapt. Ultimately, the petition failed to receive enough signatures by the filing period, and 792 went unchallenged, ready for a vote of the people during the 2016 election in November. All of the hard work from grass-roots movements to industry-led lobbyists paid off as the measure passed with 939,848 votes, a 65 percent margin of the total vote. Breweries had already enjoyed the benefits and saw a massive spike in revenue as taproom visits became a new tourist attraction in the state. Other larger corporations and businesses started filing for their licenses and making the necessary adjustments for refrigeration space and space for wine if they chose to do so. The ABLE commission was flooded with hundreds of applications from all over the state as grocers, convenience stores and new breweries were investing in a bright new future for the state of Oklahoma.

AFTERWORD

What Oklahoma lacked in brewing history, it certainly made up for the past two decades with innovative businesses and world-class breweries. As the major cities continue to grow and bring in young, forward-thinking citizens, the brewing scene has continued to grow and prosper. Beer is ever-changing in trends and flavors while being more inclusive than ever before. It has been exciting to see how Oklahoma brewers influence these dynamic times now that they are on the same level as the rest of the country. As the gates of opportunity were opened wide, many of the new laws wouldn't take effect until October 1, 2018. This was to give stores ample time to sell off stock of low-point beer and prepare to expand into cold refrigeration and wine sales if they chose to do so. Liquor is still only allowed to be sold at liquor stores. However, breweries can apply for a mixed drinks license and serve other items like wine and cider.

In 2015, there were several breweries "in planning" that were all dialing in their recipes, promoting themselves at local beer festivals and selling swag to raise capital for the eventual legislation change. Around 2016, a brewery in the United States was opening almost every 1.5 business days. Oklahoma contributed to that figure when the average of five breweries opened each year since the law changes of 2016. Many were preparing for the legislation to be voted on and opened up taprooms to cash in on the new business structure. It became the new Tulsa oil boom of 1905, as more places opened not just in major cities but also in the surrounding towns, where

Afterword

neighborhood breweries became the new trend. One such was Renaissance Brewing Company, opened by Glenn Hall right in his neighborhood with the same name. He literally built up his residence at the corner of Twelfth and Lewis in Tulsa with his own capital. Glenn was an avid homebrewer, and after a sixteen-year career in IT, he took his hobby seriously when he attended the Siebel Institute in Chicago to become a professional brewer. He learned of German beer culture from his time as an exchange student in high school to studying a few semesters in college. Glenn adopted the German style to his line of brewing, with an Oklahoma flair with beers like Renaissance Gold, Indian Wheat and Black Gold.

Another Siebel graduate we mentioned earlier in the book, Austin McIlroy, created Cabin Boys Brewing Company in Tulsa during the fall of 2017. Trained in Germany, Austin brewed several Belgian-style beers with flavors represented in Oklahoma. His wife, Lisa, utilized her artistic talents for the packaging and branding. They operated under the slogan "Crafted for Community," which is a philosophy that a lot of these breweries started to implement. The name originated from a family cabin near Catoosa, Oklahoma, and Austin developed several Belgian-style beers, including a tripel called the Bearded Theologian, a Belgian quad and eventually an award-winning beer with their Belgian single, Goin' Stag.

Just down from Tenth and Broadway in Oklahoma City, Twisted Spike Brewing started with eight beers on tap as the newest addition to Automobile Alley in late 2016. Its 4.5 percent crisp and lightly fruited kolsch, Crew, was the first offering. The TSB IPA dry hopped with Citra, Centennial and Amarillo is a smooth, easy drinker brewed as a West Coast style. The Black Snake imperial stout is a pleasant surprise with some dark fruit and raisin notes followed by chocolate roast in the finish. The rustic, industrial railroad décor is perfect being located next to the tracks off Tenth Street. The glass partition lets you see what's fermenting, and a tie-dye painted wall is the backdrop for its sour beer/barrel aging program. Bruce Sanchez had won several homebrewing awards before deciding to go pro, with his wife as the head of marketing.

In the heart of Hochatown, near Broken Bow Lake, Mountain Fork Brewery opened its doors at the end of summer 2016 and has been brewing nonstop since then. Originally, five unique ales were brewed on its two-barrel system; it upgraded to a twenty-barrel system in the summer of 2017. With the addition of a canning line and small barrel program, this niche brewery has expanded distribution across the state in just a few short years. Just down the road, in the Beavers Bend State Park area, resides Beavers

Afterword

Brewer Austin McIlroy is showing Ben Birney the ropes at the Elgin Park Brewery before leaving to start his new endeavor at Cabin Boys Brewery. *Photo by the author.*

Bend Brewing. It opened its brewpub's current facility in April 2016 with a seven-barrel system. Before that, it brewed in Idabel, dating back to the fall of 2013. Beavers Bend has about seven staple beers brewed on site and several seasonals.

A highly anticipated brewery opened to the public on July 15, 2017. Stonecloud Brewing opened its doors to a crowd waiting to try its barrel-aged sours, IPAs and stouts. Owner Joel Irby had been planning this venture for the previous three years while he was working over at Avery Brewing in Colorado. "Working with the Pivot Project and taking on the renovation of the Sunshine Laundry building was a huge task. Being a part of the revitalization of downtown Oklahoma City is very important to me. I truly want to have an active role in the Oklahoma craft beer movement, as well as being involved with local businesses and organizations in the Oklahoma City community. That sense of working together and bonding is what really makes brewing a labor of love," said Joel. They took over the former Sunshine Laundry & Cleaners building and renovated it into a brewery, office space

Afterword

and potential space for a restaurant. The first beer brewed on Stonecloud's system was the Neon Sunshine, a medium-bodied, hazy witbier with notes of citrus and a tart finish. It has a multitude of barrels for aging adjunct-heavy stouts and sour ales like its Journey Home, an apricot sour ale brewed with apricots, Brett, Lacto and Pedio and aged in red wine barrels.

High Gravity Fermentations, which is already an icon in the state for what it contributes to the brewing world, opened Pippin's Taproom in 2017. Owner Dave Knott builds electronic brew systems that ship worldwide alongside his wife, Desiree, who runs the retail operations. With their newest location in south Tulsa, a taproom was inevitable. They started with six different beers, all at 4 percent and under, but worked to obtain their full-strength liquor license due to the archaic laws still in place. Regardless of high ABV, this crew hand-crafts beers true to style even with the low-alcohol restrictions, like the Itsy Bitsy IPA, a session IPA brewed with hops imparting grapefruit and citrus flavors. Currently, High Gravity has more than twelve beers on tap, distributing to local retailers, and it also runs the Tulsa Craft Beer Invitational beer tasting.

The much-anticipated Heirloom Rustic Ales opened its doors on November 17 in the Kendall Whittier District to a crowd that appreciates real artisanal ales focused on locally sourced ingredients with impactful flavors—like sweet potatoes from Progressive Farm and Dry Creek Refuge for its beer Pocahaunted, a fall mild beer that also incorporates Oklahoma sorghum. In the space you'll indulge on these beers, Jake Miller stated, "We're trying to cultivate a culture at our brewery. We want people to come to our space and stay a while. We'll be showing old-school skate and hip hop videos on our projector; the beers will be focused on being refreshing, complex and diverse; and the aesthetic is charming and inviting." These are table beers with dominating flavors, and alcohol is a second fiddle. Jake Miller poetically crafts these beers with Zach and Melissa French, as they have a passion for locally sourced ingredients and supporting Oklahoma's rich agriculture.

After taprooms became the rage, Ponca City welcomed Vortex Alley Brewing to its downtown, offering a rotating six taps to what the four owners saw fit. They operate on a 1.5-barrel brew system that allows them to brew a wide spectrum of beers, from their Mobrewition Cream Ale to Costa Coffee Stout. "If I had to brew the same beer over and over again, I'd probably lose my mind. I like to venture out and try new things. We'll always have some kind of IPA and possibly a smoked beer because we love that style," commented David Thomas, co-owner and public

Afterword

relations manager. Likewise, a gose will always be on, with different fruit varieties like a cherry limeade version. These gents literally hand-built their taproom, from the barstools to the bar tops and signage. One iconic piece is their main bar top, with their name water-cut out and filled with hops and different color grains. They've created an approachable place that will soon become the new neighborhood bar where you can enjoy a pint or take a growler home with you.

As you can see from these breweries, there truly was potential around the state from entrepreneurs who wanted to bring their philosophy of brewing to Oklahoma. While some had trained outside of the state, they saw the untapped market rich with potential and built up a long-lost industry. Then there's the amount of tax revenue they would bring into the state. As of 2020, there were roughly sixty breweries that brought in close to $700 million of economic impact to the state—not to mention the numerous bars, restaurants and related businesses that thrive on selling local beer to their patrons. Education became more of a selling point as breweries tapped into new styles, each one doing something a little different than the other. A new generation of drinkers with more disposable income also helped spark a level of interest in trying the latest trend of hazy IPAs, sour beers and pastry stouts. Breweries became destination points, and as more opened, people made day trips focused around brewery hopping. Despite hardships and adversity, brewing in Oklahoma has been restored to a vital industry, with much more room to grow. I can't wait to see what comes sweeping down the plains next.

Appendix
OKLAHOMA BREWERY DIRECTORY

American Solera
1702 East Sixth Street
Tulsa, OK 74104
americansolera.com

Angry Scotsman Brewing
704 West Reno Avenue
Oklahoma City, OK 73102
angryscotbrew.com

Anthem Brewing
908 Southwest Fourth Street
Oklahoma City, OK 73109
anthembrewing.com

Battered Boar Brewing Company
14700 Metro Plaza Boulevard, Suite F
Edmond, OK 73013
batteredboar.com

Beavers Bend Brewery
46 Coho Road
Broken Bow, OK 74728
beaversbendbrewery.com

Appendix

Beer Is Good Brewing Company
216 East Main Street
Norman, OK 73069
bigbrew.co

Belle Isle Restaurant & Brewery
1900 Northwest Expressway, #44R
Oklahoma City, OK 73118
belleislerestaurant.com

Bierkraft
925 East Washington Avenue
McAlester, OK 74501
bierkraft.us

The Big Friendly
1737 Spoke Street
Oklahoma City, OK 73108
thebigfriendly.com

Black Mesa Brewing Company
3901 North Flood Avenue
Norman, OK 73069
blackmesabrewing.com

Bricktown Brewery
1 North Oklahoma Avenue
Oklahoma City, OK 73104
bricktownbrewery.com

Broke Brewing Company
3810 North Tulsa Avenue, Suite Z
Oklahoma City, OK 73112
broke.beer

Broken Arrow Brewing Company
333 West Dallas Street
Broken Arrow, OK 74012
brokenarrowbrewingco.com

Appendix

Cabin Boys Brewery
1717 East Seventh Street
Tulsa, OK 74104
cabinboysbrewery.com

Canadian River Brewing Company
121 West Chickasha Avenue
Chickasha, OK 73018
canadianriverbrewingco.com

The Cape Brewing Company
732 West Main Street
Jenks, OK 74037
thecapebrewingcompany.com

COOP Ale Works
4745 Council Heights Road
Oklahoma City, OK 73179

Cooper & Mill Brewing Company
200 Dewey Avenue
Bartlesville, OK 74003
cooperandmill.com

Core4 Brewing Company
7 North Lee Avenue
Oklahoma City, OK 73102
core4brewing.square.site

Crossed Cannons Brewery
333 West Boyd Street
Norman, OK 73069
crossedcannonsbrewery.square.site

Cross Timbers Brewing
520 North Meridian Avenue
Oklahoma City, OK 73142

Appendix

Dead Armadillo Brewery
1004 East Fourth Street
Tulsa, OK 74120
dabrewery.com

Dollhouse Road Brewing
301 West Main Street
Pawhuska, OK 74056
taplist.io/dollhouseroad

Downstream Crafted Brewing at Downstream Casino & Resort
69300 East Nee Road
Quapaw, OK 74363
downstreamcasino.com

Eerie Abbey Ales
507 South Main Street
Tulsa, OK 74103
eerieabbeyales.com

Elgin Park Brewery
325 East Reconciliation Way
Tulsa, OK 74120
elginparkbrewery.com

Elk Valley Brewing
1212 North Hudson Avenue
Oklahoma City, OK 73103
elkvalleybrew.com

Emersumnice Brewery
102 South Main Street, Suite E
Owasso, OK 74055
emersumnicebrewery.com

Enid Brewing Company & Eatery
126 South Independence Avenue
Enid, OK 73701
enidbrewing.com

Appendix

Equity Brewing Company
109 East Tonhawa Street, Suite 100
Norman, OK 73069
equitybrewingco.com

Expenditure Brewery
201 South Second Street
Okarche, OK 73762
expedinturebrewery.com

Fair-Weather Friend
314 North Klein Avenue
Oklahoma City, OK 73106
fwfbeer.com

Fat Toad Brewing Company
3986 West 530 Road
Pryor, OK 74103
fattoadbrewing.com

(405) Brewing Company
1716 Topeka Street
Norman, OK 73069
405brewing.com

Frenzy Brewing Company
15 South Broadway
Edmond, OK 73034
frenzybrewing.com

Harbinger Beer Company
111 Buffalo Street
Caddo, OK 74729
harbingerbeer.com

Heirloom Rustic Ales
2113 East Admiral Boulevard
Tulsa, OK 74110
heirloomrusticales.com

Appendix

High Gravity Fermentations and Pippin's Taproom
6808 South Memorial Drive, Suite 144
Tulsa, OK 74133
highgravitybrewingco.com

Iron Monk
519 South Husband
Stillwater, OK 74074
ironmonkbeer.com

Kochendorfer Brewing Company
1155 McCurdy Road
Duncan, OK 73533
kochendorferbrewing.com

Lazy Circles Brewing
422 East Main Street
Norman, OK 73071
lazycirclesbrewing.com

Lively Beerworks
815 Southwest Second Street
Oklahoma City, OK 73109
livelybeerworks.com

Lost Street Brewing Company
109 Lost Street
Durant, OK 74701
loststreetbrewing.com

Marshall Brewing Company
618 South Wheeling Avenue
Tulsa, OK 74104
marshallbrewing.com

Mountain Fork Brewery
85 North Lukfata Trail Road
Broken Bow, OK 74728
mtforkbrewery.com

Appendix

MUSKOGEE BREWING COMPANY
121 South Second Street
Muskogee, OK 74401
muskogeebrewingcompany.com

NEFF BREWING
321 South Frankfort Avenue
Tulsa, OK 74120
neffbrewing.com

THE NOOK BREWING COMPANY
909 South Twelfth Street
Broken Arrow, OK 74012
nookbrewco.com

NOTHING'S LEFT BREWING COMPANY
1501 East Sixth Street
Tulsa, OK 74120
nothingsleftbrew.co

OK CIDER COMPANY
705 West Sheridan Avenue
Oklahoma City, OK 73102
okciderco.com

PRAIRIE ARTISAN ALES
3 Northeast Eighth Street
Oklahoma City, OK 73104
prairieales.com

RAPTURE BREWING
24962 West 141st Street S
Kellyville, OK 74039
https://www.facebook.com/rapturebrewing

RENAISSANCE BREWING COMPANY
1147 South Lewis Avenue
Tulsa, OK 74104
renaissancebeer.com

Appendix

The River Brewhouse
Tahlequah, OK 74464
theriverbrewhouse.com

Roughtail Brewing Company
320 West Memorial Road
Oklahoma City, OK 73114
roughtailbeer.com

Royal Bavaria
3401 South Sooner Road
Oklahoma City, OK 73165
royal-bavaria.com

Scissortail Brewing Company
623 East Don Tyler
Dewey, OK 74029
scissortailbrew.com

Settlers Brewing Company
202 East Randolph Avenue
Enid, OK 73701
settlersbrewingco.com

SneakyTiki Restaurant and Brewery
3263 US 70
Mead, OK 73449
laketexomalodge.com

Stonecloud Brewing Company
1012 Northwest First Street
Oklahoma City, OK 73106
stonecloudbrewing.com

Twisted Spike Brewing Company
1 Northwest Tenth Street
Oklahoma City, OK 73103
twistedspike.com

Appendix

Vanessa House Beer Company
118 Northwest Eighth Street
Oklahoma City, OK 73102
vanessahousebeerco.com

Vortex Alley Brewing
220 East Central Avenue
Ponca City, OK 74601
vortexalleybrewing.com

War Pony Brewing Company (Comanche Nation Casino)
402 Southeast Interstate Drive
Lawton, OK 73501
comanchenationcasino.com

Welltown Brewing Company
114 West Archer Street
Tulsa, OK 74103

Winnicki Brewing Company
7113 Northwest Eightieth Street, Suite 6
Oklahoma City, OK 73132
winnickibrewing.com

BIBLIOGRAPHY

Regarding to the publication Southwest Brewing News, *which covered craft brewing in the southwest portion of the United States since the early '90s, specific articles are not listed in the interest of saving space. All articles are digitally archived and in the author's possession.*

"AAA: Relatives of Creators Helped Restore Old Recipe." *Daily Oklahoman*, July 4, 2012, 72.
"Ahrens Brewery Ready to Function." *Tulsa Daily World*, August 10, 1938, 1–8.
Alcott, Matt. "Empty Mug." *Tulsa World*, November 10, 1998. https://www.tulsaworld.com/archive/empty-mug/article_327809a5-0122-5b49-af75-81ed847b4189.html.
Averill, Ellen. "Brew Pub Marks First Year." *Tulsa World*, August 17, 1994.
———. "Cherry Street Brewery Gets New Operator." *Tulsa World*, June 3, 1994. https://tulsaworld.com/archive/cherry-street-brewery-gets-new-operator/article_023f3ca9-fe75-5365-b49e-f38e9b5bedc8.html.
Averill, Mike. "Marshall Brewing to Unveil Spring Seasonal Revival Red Ale." *Tulsa World*, March 3, 2011. https://tulsaworld.com/archive/marshall-brewing-to-unveil-spring-seasonal-revival-red-ale/article_2c39491d-7b8b-5af7-8bf4-f8a14c1adbce.html.
———. "New Marshall Brew to Debut at First Draft." *Tulsa World*, November 3, 2010. https://tulsaworld.com/lifestyles/food-and-cooking/new-marshall-brew-to-debut-at-first-draft/article_37eb6b2b-e440-5ab9-acf2-421cdbcb802e.html.

Bibliography

Bailey, Brianna. "Beer Conflict Brewing." *Daily Oklahoman*, August 20, 2016, 17, 22.

Ball, Natasha. "Brewmaster Releases Oktoberfest-Style Beer." *Tulsa World*, September 12, 2009. https://tulsaworld.com/archive/brewmaster-releases-oktoberfest-style-beer/article_2043e15a-a12d-5119-b21b-0e7313869bb0.html.

———. "Six-Pack City." *Tulsa World*, December 16, 2010. https://tulsaworld.com/archive/six-pack-city/article_3d0e4eff-49af-575f-aab7-778e421e87ce.html.

"The Ban Is on Choctaw Beer." *Muskogee Times-Democrat*, August 22, 1912, 2.

"The Big Brewing House Will Be Heavily Financed." *Daily Oklahoman*, April 12, 1902, 1.

"Beer and Oil." *Daily Oklahoman*, August 25, 1944, 12.

"Beer Goes into the Ditch at 2 Today." *Daily Oklahoman*, August 27, 1908, 1.

"Beer Industries Launch Attack in Local Option." *Daily Oklahoman*, October 4, 1957, 43.

"Beer Industry Getting All Set to Battle Drys." *Daily Oklahoman*, October 28, 1955, 20.

"Beer Worth $8,000 Poured into Oklahoma City Sewer." *Daily Oklahoman*, August 28, 1908, 1.

"Beer-Lovers Open Brewpubs in U.S." *Daily Oklahoman*, May 28, 1987, 50.

"Begins Work on Brewery." *Daily Times-Journal*. November 20, 1900, 5.

"Bottled Beer on the Market." *Daily Oklahoman*, January 31, 1904, 5.

"Brewers Will Not Fight Enforcement of New Law." *Daily Oklahoman*, September 21, 1907, 5.

"Brewery Adds to Plant, Sees New Expansion." *Daily Oklahoman*, July 12, 1964, 64.

"Brewing Measure Signed." *Daily Oklahoman*, April 25, 1992, 90.

"Business Leaders Expect Many Good Days Ahead." *Daily Oklahoman*, January 1, 1937, 8.

Canfield, Kevin. "Planning Commission Backs Zoning Change for Pearl District Micro Brewery." *Tulsa World*, August 21, 2014. https://tulsaworld.com/news/local/planning-commission-backs-zoning-change-for-pearl-district-micro-brewery/article_37dfd58f-1d8b-56e7-8be5-c1022ef92ed3.html.

Cathey, Dave. "It's a Brand New Bricktown Brewery." *Daily Oklahoman*, January 12, 2012, 8D.

Bibliography

———. "The Legend of Krebs Begins with Pete's Place." *Daily Oklahoman*, October 11, 2012, 80.

———. "Year One of the COOP Empire." *Daily Oklahoman*, January 6, 2010, 99, 101.

"Chain Acquires City Brewery." *Daily Oklahoman*, June 2, 1946, 1.

Cherry, Scott. "House Kills Sampling Bill for Oklahoma Breweries." *Tulsa World*, March 21, 2012. https://tulsaworld.com/entertainment/house-kills-sampling-bill-for-oklahoma-breweries/article_63b9329e-6832-5b94-bc85-01cf82ae6f1d.html.

———. "Roughtail to Bring 5 Beers to Annual McNellie's Festival." *Tulsa World*, September 19, 2013. https://tulsaworld.com/lifestyles/food-and-cooking/roughtail-to-bring-5-beers-to-annual-mcnellies-festival/article_67b2e58b-64f6-5a9d-b9ea-6e09ddc1ecf3.html.

———. "Tulsa Brewers Dead Armadillo Bursting at Seams, Ready for Craft Beer Week." *Tulsa World*, April 6, 2014. https://tulsaworld.com/entertainment/dining/tulsa-brewers-dead-armadillo-bursting-at-seams-ready-for-craft-beerweekarticle_a9e34d23-4c48-55aa-aa9f-d295dd7bce7c.html.

"Choc Beats Real Beer, Aver 'Fans' Who've Tried the Brew." *Muskogee Times-Democrat*, August 12, 1919, 2.

"Choctaw Beer and Statesmanship." *Daily Ardmoreite*, May 3, 1915, 7.

"City Brewery Sale Is Completed." *Daily Oklahoman*, June 7, 1946, 2.

Cleary, Paul. "The Last Dry State." *OK Magazine* (1979): 7.

"Clubs or Pubs?" *Daily Oklahoman*, August 23, 1959, 16.

Conner, Thomas. "Satisfy Your Thirst (& Your Soul) at Once." *Tulsa World*, June 6, 1997. https://www.tulsaworld.com/archive/satisfy-your-thirst-your-soul-at-once/article_da757c46-4063-5f4a-b6ff-9d9966c5022b.html.

"Craft Brewers on Hold as New Law Gets Vetted." *Daily Oklahoman*, August 23, 2016, 8.

Culver, Harry. "Beer Industry 'Protecting Self' on Petition." *Sapulpa Daily Herald*, September 24, 1969, 1.

———. "Oklahoma's Beer Industry Hops into By-the-Drink Petition Brew." *Tulsa Daily World*, September 24, 1969.

Daily Oklahoman. Digital Images, April 23, 1939, 247.

———. Digital Images, January 15, 1939, 35.

———. Digital Images, July 29, 1906, 12.

———. Digital Images, March 7, 1905, 3.

———. Digital Images, March 13, 1906, 12.

———. Digital Images, September 23, 1934, 35.

Bibliography

"Damage in City Warehouse Fire Near $75,000." *Daily Oklahoman*, November 13, 1948, 27.

David, Amy. "Beer Garden Brews Debate." *Daily Oklahoman*, July 17, 1996, 77.

"Death Comes at 79 for John F. Kroutil." *Daily Oklahoman*, June 13, 1954, 24.

Dees, Cynthia. "Tulsa 'Brewpub' Set to Open October 1 // Shopping Center Gets Tenants." *Tulsa World*, July 8, 1993. https://www.tulsaworld.com/archive/tulsa-brewpub-set-to-open-oct-1-shopping-center-gets-tenants/article_4a360cd1-e6ad-525f-9920-4f215c325049.html.

DeFrange, Steve. "This Old Ice House." *Oklahoma Heritage* (Winter 1999): 18–23.

Denton, Jon. "Interurban Brewing Up New Appeal, Own Beer." *Daily Oklahoman*, May 29, 1994, 37.

———. "MAPS Inspires Expansion Plan for Brew-Pub." *Daily Oklahoman*, January 30, 1994, 39, 42.

———. "Norman Brewery Expanding." *Daily Oklahoman*, August 7, 1994, 70.

———. "Serving Up Grid Legends." *Daily Oklahoman*, July 28, 1996, 37.

Dowell, Sharon. "Bricktown Brewery to Feature 'New Prairie' Cooking." *Daily Oklahoman*, August 26, 1992, 19.

Downing, Jim. "Drinking Wet, Voting Dry." *Tulsa Tribune*, April 11, 1979, 7B.

"Dry Challenged to Prove Beer, Repeal Linked." *Daily Oklahoman*, October 5, 1957, 16.

"Dry-Up Drive Spurring Beer Sale in State." *Daily Oklahoman*, February 17, 1959, 7.

"18-Year-Old Sooner Males May Buy Beer." *Tulsa Daily World*, December 20, 1970, A-1.

"Election Set for July 11 in 28-15 Ballot." *Daily Oklahoman*, April 13, 1933, 1.

Ervin, Chuck. "State Plans Strict Drinking Policy." *Tulsa World*, April 23, 1985, A-1, 4.

———. "Writing Drink Bill Was Sobering Task." *Tulsa World*, July 1, 1985, 1.

Evans, Trisha. "Old World Flair Draws Favor for Brew Master." *Daily Oklahoman*, November 3, 2007, 20.

Evatt, Robert. "Local Craft Beers Tapping into Success." *Tulsa World*, July 29, 2010. https://tulsaworld.com/business/local-craft-beers-tapping-into-success/article_9c126425-f70f-5bcc-a0ee-87b445360da6.html.

"A $50,000 Fire." *Daily Oklahoman*, December 23, 1905, 3.

Bibliography

"Final Ballot Fate of Bill Is Uncertain." *Daily Oklahoman*, April 11, 1933, 1.

"40 Under 40: Wes Alexander, 35." *Tulsa World*, June 7, 2010. https://tulsaworld.com/archive/40-under-40-wes-alexander-35/article_706f8e68-bd79-5dec-a0eb-13863046eead.html.

"Gary's Needled on Beer Issue." *Daily Oklahoman*, April 8, 1956, 79.

"German Brew-Pub Launched." *Daily Oklahoman*, February 27, 1994, 44.

Gilbert, Tom. "American Solera Named Best New Brewery in U.S.; Announces New Location at 18th and Boston." *Tulsa World*, January 31, 2017. https://tulsaworld.com/lifestyles/food-and-cooking/american-solera-named-best-new-brewery-in-u-s-announces-newlocation-at-18th-and/article_38bd9dcb-5a97-546d-b84a-3e15ac065025.html.

———. "Hanson Launches Mmmhops Beer from Oklahoma's Mustang Brewing." *Tulsa World*, May 29, 2013. https://tulsaworld.com/entertainment/hanson-launches-mmmhops-beer-from-oklahomas-mustangbrewing/article_edb10d5a-60ef-5973-bfc2-c16f404df6fd.html.

———. "New Brewpub Across from ONEOK Field Planned to Open Next Year." *Tulsa World*, August 14, 2014. https://tulsaworld.com/lifestyles/food-and-cooking/new-brewpub-across-from-oneok-field-planned-to-open-nextyeararticle_cb9e6b4d-3e95-5bf0-beb3-fb78e054a068.html.

———. "What the Ale: The Bomb! Is Dropping Wednesday from Prairie Artisan Ales." *Tulsa World*, January 21, 2014. https://tulsaworld.com/lifestyles/food-and-cooking/what-the-ale-the-bomb-is-dropping-wednesday-from-prairie-artisanales/article_3c790788-82d0-11e3-8a65-0019bb30f31a.html.

———. "What the Ale: Brewmaster Chase Healey's Next Project: American Solera." *Tulsa World*, July 24, 2016. https://tulsaworld.com/lifestyles/food-and-cooking/what-the-ale-brewmaster-chase-healeys-next-project-americansolera/article_187dbd24-82d6-56a4-b67b-bec52aa609ca.html.

———. "What the Ale: Choc Beer Co Gets New Tanks." *Tulsa World*, October 31, 2013. https://tulsaworld.com/lifestyles/food-and-cooking/what-the-ale-choc-beer-co-gets-new-tanks/article_87533fae-4279-11e3-b826-001a4bcf6878.html.

———. "What the Ale: Choc Beer Company in Krebs Soon to Be the Largest State Brewery." *Tulsa World*, October 16, 2013. https://tulsaworld.com/lifestyles/food-and-cooking/what-the-ale-choc-beer-company-in-krebs-soon-to-be-the-largest-statebreweryarticle_98720bb8-3698-11e3-aba6-001a4bcf6878.html.

Bibliography

———. "What the Ale: Dead Armadillo Has a Tulsa Location for New Brewery." *Tulsa World*, July 18, 2014. https://tulsaworld.com/lifestyles/food-and-cooking/what-the-ale-dead-armadillo-has-a-tulsa-location-for-new-brewery/article_715b0a14-8a6f-5ce9-bcf5-2d0be6b6142c.html.

———. "What the Ale: Hanson Brothers Beer Co., Dead Armadillo Collaborate on Beer." *Tulsa World*, March 9, 2016. https://tulsaworld.com/lifestyles/food-and-cooking/what-the-ale-hanson-brothers-beer-co-dead-armadillo-collaborate-on-beer/article_df0db27b-82b6-589e-8f39-a459b082fcac.html.

———. "What the Ale: Marshall Brewing Co. Selling Beer at the Brewery." *Tulsa World*, November 12, 2014. https://tulsaworld.com/lifestyles/food-and-cooking/what-the-ale-marshall-brewing-co-selling-beer-at-thebreweryarticle_9ab217ea-2e4c-5bae-a059-c72a76fc76cb.html.

———. "What the Ale: Mustang Brewery Moving All Its Operations to Oklahoma." *Tulsa World*, February 25, 2015. https://tulsaworld.com/lifestyles/food-and-cooking/what-the-ale-mustang-brewery-moving-all-its-operations-tooklahomaarticle_efa19b24-8c9b-5a40-b215-f6b2c18d6a47.html.

———. "What the Ale: Mustang Ready to Brew in New Brewhouse." *Tulsa World*, April 16, 2014. https://tulsaworld.com/lifestyles/food-and-cooking/what-the-ale-mustang-ready-to-brew-in-newbrewhousearticle_6204626a-c5a9-11e3-8160-0017a43b2370.html.

———. "What the Ale: Mustang to Open New Brewhouse." *Tulsa World*, November 4, 2013. https://tulsaworld.com/lifestyles/food-and-cooking/what-the-ale-mustang-to-open-new-brewhouse/article_77d8e2d4-45a0-11e3-99c0-001a4bcf6878.html.

———. "What the Ale: OKC's Mustang Brewing Co. Soon to Be Back in the Saddle." *Tulsa World*, February 25, 2014. https://tulsaworld.com/lifestyles/food-and-cooking/what-the-ale-okcs-mustang-brewing-co-soon-to-be-back-in-thesaddlearticle_3999c04a-9e4e-11e3-9a48-001a4bcf6878.html.

———. "What the Ale: Oklahoma's Largest Brewery Expands, Will Open Taprooms in McAlester, OKC." *Tulsa World*, June 12, 2017. https://tulsaworld.com/lifestyles/food-and-cooking/what-the-ale-oklahomas-largest-brewery-expands-will-open-taprooms-inmcalester-okc/article_bd20d925-9085-5eb8-ad0a-621ec0f9ab12.html.

———. "What the Ale: Prairie Artisan Ales Brewing New Brews in Tulsa." *Tulsa World*, December 18, 2013. https://tulsaworld.com/lifestyles/food-and-cooking/what-the-ale-prairie-artisan-ales-brewing-new-brews-intulsa/article_fc61f1ec-682a-11e3-ad2e-0019bb30f31a.html.

Bibliography

———. "What the Ale: Prairie Artisan Ales Brings Home Five Medals from RateBeer Awards." *Tulsa World*, February 3, 2016. https://tulsaworld.com/lifestyles/food-and-cooking/what-the-ale-prairie-artisan-ales-brings-home-five-medals-from-ratebeer-awards/article_f7b94a35-8f87-57ff-9100-dcd11673b07d.html.

———. "What the Ale: Prairie Artisan Ales First Brewery Tour in Tulsa." *Tulsa World*, December 23, 2013. https://tulsaworld.com/lifestyles/food-and-cooking/what-the-ale-prairie-artisan-ales-first-brewery-tour-intulsa/article_3972db0c-6c20-11e3-83d7-0019bb30f31a.html.

———. "What the Ale: Prairie Artisan Ales Named Top 100 by RateBeer." *Tulsa World*, January 30, 2015. https://tulsaworld.com/lifestyles/food-and-cooking/what-the-ale-prairie-artisan-ales-named-top-100-byratebeer/article_c8cfb2bf-1585-564c-8ac5-12f4d3627a85.html.

———. "What the Ale: Prairie Artisan Ales Plans New Location." *Tulsa World*, March 7, 2014. https://tulsaworld.com/lifestyles/food-and-cooking/what-the-ale-prairie-artisan-ales-plans-new-location/article_2e338daca651-11e3-8e07-001a4bcf6878.html.

———. "What the Ale: Recovery from May Storms Is Slow but Starting for Oklahoma City Breweries." *Tulsa World*, August 2, 2013. https://tulsaworld.com/archive/what-the-ale-recovery-from-may-storms-is-slow-but-starting-for-oklahoma-citybreweriesarticle_0b674198-634c-5e6f-8765-89ba8b4b184a.html.

———. "What the Ale: Status Update on Prairie Artisan Ales Tulsa Brewery." *Tulsa World*, September 11, 2013. https://tulsaworld.com/lifestyles/food-and-cooking/what-the-ale-status-update-on-prairie-artisan-ales-tulsabrewery/article_c4ec1458-8083-57fa-906f-4d485c8aca33.html.

"Government Now Has Big Brewery." *Daily Oklahoman*, June 5, 1908, 5.

"The Great Oklahoma Beer Run." *Southwestern Brewing News* (October 1995): 30.

Greene, Wayne. "Wayne Greene: Oklahoma's Long History of Prohibition in Six Shots." *Tulsa World*, September 21, 2018. https://tulsaworld.com/opinion/columnists/wayne-greene-oklahomas-long-history-of-prohibition-in-six-shots/article_a9f04258-6840-5ccc-ba2b-f1da47bde2a0.html.

Gurley, George. "Ada City Council Passes Ordinances on Private Clubs, Beer and Minors." *Ada Weekly News*, January 9, 1969, 2.

"Handling Choc a Dangerous Pasttime." *Indian Journal*, November 28, 1913, 1.

Bibliography

"Here's How to Deal with Honky-Tonks!" *Daily Oklahoman*, September 18, 1942, 13.

Hinton, Mick. "House Says No to 'Brew Pub' Bill." *NewsOK*, March 5, 1992.

Hirsch, J.M. "Hanson Hops from Singing MMMBop to Brewing Their Own Beer." *Tulsa World*, December 1, 2015. https://tulsaworld.com/lifestyles/food-and-cooking/hanson-hops-from-singing-mmmbop-to-brewing-their-ownbeer/article_30ecce7f-71b5-5f16-a533-e8a36c07c463.html.

Holloway, Suzanne. "Things Are Finally Hoppin' at Cherry Street Brewery." *Tulsa World*, December 24, 1993.

Horton, Greg. "The Brewhouse." July 2013. http://www.ionok.com/bon-appetit/the-brewhouse-2.

Hubbell, Diana. "How a Band of Brewers Got Together to Change Oklahoma's Liquor Laws." *Tulsa World*, October 23, 2018.

"Is Sold Again." *Daily Oklahoman*, January 10, 1906, 3.

Johnson, Bill. "Bricktown Site of City's First Brewery Pub." *Daily Oklahoman*, September 13, 1992, 41.

Kerl, Mary Ann. "Spice of Life in Little Krebs Is Very Italian." *Daily Oklahoman*, May 31, 1998, 6.

Klein, John. "Krebs Is an Oklahoma Success Story." *Daily Oklahoman*, June 8, 2017, 5.

Knickmeyer, Naomi. "Miller Urges Bill to Clarify Oklahoma's Beer Laws." *Ada Weekly News*, March 20, 1969, 5.

"Krebs Fans Offered 2 News Bits." *Daily Oklahoman*, April 24, 1995, 85.

Krehbiel, Randy. "Strong Beer a 'No Sale.'" *Tulsa World*, December 30, 2007, A4.

Lackmeyer, Steve. "Beer-Loving Entrepreneurs Hop Head-First into Venture." *Daily Oklahoman*, February 5, 2009, 15.

———. "Coop Ale Works Official Captures Attention of Many in Oklahoma City." *Daily Oklahoman*, November 15, 2009.

———. "Drinking It Up." *Daily Oklahoman*, December 28, 2007, 19.

———. "Oklahoma City's H&8th Festival Still Trucking Along." *Daily Oklahoman*, April 29, 2014, 26.

Levy, Larry. "Lone Star Expands Again." *Daily Oklahoman*, January 1, 1967, 18.

Lewis, Jone Johnson. "Temperance Movement and Prohibition Timeline." ThoughtCo, February 16, 2021. thoughtco.com/temperance-movement-prohibition-timeline-3530548.

Bibliography

"Liquid Assets of Brewery Go in the Sewer." *Daily Oklahoman*, March 9, 1940, 75.

"Liquor Board's Cash Chopped." *Daily Oklahoman*, June 11, 1959, 1.

"Local Thirsts Will Grow; 'Choc' Placed Under Same Ban as Fierce 'White Mule.'" *Daily Oklahoman*, September 23, 1915, 5.

"Lone Star Closing Its City Brewery." *Daily Oklahoman*, January 28, 1971, 61.

"Lone Star Stock Buys Progress Beer Assets." *Daily Oklahoman*, March 11, 1960, 50.

Malone, Paul Scott. "Gentleman's Agreement Keeps 'Choc' Beer Flowing." *Tulsa World*, August 17, 1971, 1, 13.

Malone, Tara. "Easy or Hard to Swallow." OKMag, August 27, 2018.

"Mammonth Brewery Plant." *Daily Ardmoreite*, October 2, 1902, 7.

"Marshall Brewing Co. Expands Capacity." *Tulsa World*, March 2010. https://tulsaworld.com/archive/marshall-brewing-co-expands-capacity/article_3b7acc0a-98b5-5f60-ab78-9e85cebc4b38.html.

McCleland, Jacob. "'Born Sober,' but Always Plentiful: How Oklahoma Got Its Liquor Laws." KGOU, September 29, 2016. https://www.kgou.org/politics-and-government/2016-09-29/born-sober-but-always-plentiful-how-oklahoma-got-its-liquor-laws.

Middleton, Nicole Marshall. "Artistic Inspiration Overrides Homework." *Tulsa World*, October 13, 2013. https://tulsaworld.com/entertainment/artistic-inspiration-overrides-homework/article_6c79ee04-33dc-11e3-ba5e-001a4bcf6878.html.

———. "Brewing Change: Beer Advocates Unite to Update State's Restrictive Alcohol Laws." *Tulsa World*, March 11, 2015. https://tulsaworld.com/lifestyles/food-and-cooking/brewing-change-beer-advocates-unite-to-update-states-restrictivealcohol-laws/article_bc5bb99a-9e20-5b81-a5cf-bd50bac02f2e.html.

———. "Marshall Brewing Co. to Release Arrowhead Pale Ale on Wednesday." *Tulsa World*, June 1, 2012. https://tulsaworld.com/lifestyles/food-and-cooking/marshall-brewing-co-to-release-arrowhead-pale-ale-onwednesday/article_52be863c-a9b0-575b-ae15-7b5b67994fa3.html.

———. "Oklahoma Craft Beer Brewers Continue to Flourish—Meet Them at The Hop Jam." *Tulsa World*, May 10, 2015. https://tulsaworld.com/entertainment/music/oklahoma-craft-beer-brewers-continue-to-flourish-meet-them-at-the-hop-jam/article_ab0dc462-6a27-5b9b-b312-79bab96ec8d9.html.

Bibliography

———. "Sunday: Fans of Tulsa's Prairie Artisan Ales Calling for More." *Tulsa World*, October 12, 2013. https://tulsaworld.com/lifestyles/food-and-cooking/sunday-fans-of-tulsas-prairie-artisan-ales-calling-formore/article_82156dac-3395-11e3-9963-0019bb30f31a.html.

———. "What Are You…? with Chase Healey, Brewmaster at Prairie Artisan Ales." *Tulsa World*, July 25, 2013. https://tulsaworld.com/lifestyles/food-and-cooking/what-are-you-with-chase-healey-brewmaster-at-prairie-artisanales/article_a36b8ac8-af4e-59ef-8da4-df7c4c0e722c.html.

Mikles, Natalie. "COOP Shakes Up Staff, Moves Forward on Cans." *Tulsa World*, August 18, 2010. https://tulsaworld.com/lifestyles/food-and-cooking/mustang-brewing-co-founder-finds-perseverance-paysoffarticle_5163acaf-7ffb-5487-b376-a5ce99ed6342.html.

Molina, Sarah. "Beer Law's Change Puts Hop in Sales." *Daily Oklahoman*, November 2, 2003, 8.

Morehead, Lindsey. "Marshall Brewing to Expand to Arkansas, Missouri." *Tulsa World*, March 26, 2012. https://tulsaworld.com/archive/marshall-brewing-to-expand-to-arkansas-missouri/article_086c5fd3-d07b-5dec-a8c7-2704e7596563.html.

Morgan, Kay. "Booze 'n' Beer: We Love It and We Hate It Wet-Dry War Still Raging." *Daily Oklahoman*, November 15, 1987.

Morris, Marshall. "Eric & Adam Marshall—Founders of Marshall Brewing Company." *Beer, Scales & Ales* podcast. http://madness-media.com/interview-founders-marshall-brewing-company-eric-marshall-adam-marshall-scales-ales-podcast.

"Moss Brewery Raided and Cooling Beverage Seized." *Daily Oklahoman*, June 4, 1908, 5.

"Moss Brewing Company." *Daily Oklahoman*, March 10, 1907, 85.

"Mr. Busch Will Be Made President." *Daily Oklahoman*, January 27, 1904, 13.

"Mustang Brewing Co. Takes Silver in the World Beer Championships." *Daily Oklahoman*, August 5, 2010.

Myers, Jim. "Nigh Signs Liquor-by-the-Drink Bill." *Tulsa World*, March 15, 1985, A-1, 4.

———. "Wine Coolers Spark Legal Debate." *Tulsa World*, June 21, 1987, A-1, 4.

Nelson, Lori Yost. "Authentic Italian Tastes Cooking in Krebs." *Daily Oklahoman*, December 10, 2000, 90.

"New Bottling Works Opens." *Daily Oklahoman*, March 23, 1961, 16.

Bibliography

"New Brewery Building Opens." *Daily Oklahoman*, April 30, 2014, 27.
"New State Brewery Quits Making Beer." *Daily Oklahoman*, September 26, 1907, 19.
"960 Feet Down for Beer?" *Daily Oklahoman*, October 1, 1939, 39.
"Norman Sports Bar Known as Place for Suds and Celebrity." *Tulsa World*, August 4, 1996. https://www.tulsaworld.com/archive/norman-sports-bar-known-as-place-for-suds-and-celebrity/article_b25c1c95-dee6-57e7-88d2-7da1e85ad16e.html.
"North Broadway." *Daily Oklahoman*, March 13, 1903, 3.
"Oklahoma Beer Measure as Finally Passed." *Daily Oklahoman*, April 14, 1933, 12.
"Oklahoma City Beermaker Unveils State-of-the-Art Brewery Building." *Daily Oklahoman*, April 30, 2014.
"Oklahoma City Brewery, Now Building." *Daily Oklahoman*, March 22, 1903, 11.
"Oklahoma Panhandle: Badmen in No Man's Land." HistoryNet. https://www.historynet.com/oklahoma-panhandle-badmen-in-no-mans-land.htm.
"Oklahoma's Great Brewery." *Daily Oklahoman*, February 28, 1904, 28.
"One-Year-Old City Brewery Hires Sixty." *Daily Oklahoman*, March 8, 1936, 20.
Overall, Michael. "Hops for Tulsa." *Tulsa World*, October 9, 2007.
———. "Law Change Makes Free Samples Legal at Oklahoma Breweries." *Tulsa World*, October 30, 2013. https://tulsaworld.com/news/local/law-change-makes-free-samples-legal-at-oklahoma-breweries/article_de41e6ac-41d5-11e3-8e8a-0019bb30f31a.html.
Parr, Ray. "Battle Brewing for City Option." *Daily Oklahoman*, February 24, 1959, 33.
———. "State Election on Beer Repeal Voted by House." *Daily Oklahoman*, April 1, 1953, 29.
Percefull, Gary. "Before Liquor Laws—The Good Ole Days?" *Tulsa World*, July 1, 1985, 7.
Postelwait, Jeff. "Here's to Tulsa." *Tulsa World*, June 4, 2008. https://tulsaworld.com/business/retail/heres-to-tulsa/article_b0783dd5-727a-5d8e-9888-21e129b242c2.html.
"Price List Filed for Strong Beer." *Daily Oklahoman*, August 22, 1959, 10.
"Progress Brewing Executives Bring Business, Technical Experience to New Firm." *Daily Oklahoman*, April 7, 1935, Section A-F.
"Prohibition Law Points Settled." *Daily Oklahoman*, May 11, 1910, 10.

Bibliography

"Receiver's Sale." *Daily Oklahoman*, November 12, 1905, 8.

"Restaurateur Dies at 64." *Daily Oklahoman*, October 5, 1994, 8.

Ridenour, Windsor. "Open Beer Can in Car Becomes Illegal Tuesday." *Tulsa Tribune*, 1969, 1.

"Senate Makes Full Redraft of State's Beer Measure." *Daily Oklahoman*, April 8, 1933, 2.

"Senate Votes $10 Beer Tax." *Daily Oklahoman*, March 9, 1945, 2.

Sewell, Steven L. "Choctaw Beer: Tonic or Devil's Brew?" *Journal of Cultural Geography* 23, no. 2 (2006): 105–15.

"Showdown Near On Liquor Tax." *Daily Oklahoman*, June 3, 1959, 34.

"Sooner Beer Firm Is Sold." *Daily Oklahoman*, October 3, 1959, 11.

"Southwest Brewing Corporation First to Offer Native Beer." *Daily Oklahoman*, February 25, 1934, 2-D.

"Special Officer May Smash All Near Beers." *Daily Oklahoman*, September 17, 1907, 10.

"Speedy Hearings on Liquor Bill Due." *Daily Oklahoman*, April 21, 1959, 25.

"St. Louis Party." *Daily Oklahoman*, April 11, 1906, 5.

"Stabs at State in Liquor Trial." *Daily Oklahoman*, September 29, 1908, 8.

Stafford, Jim. "Entrepreneur Recalls Start, Winning '08 Governor's Cup." *Daily Oklahoman*, November 2, 2014, 42.

———. "Oklahoma's Black Mesa Brewing Uses Science to Brew Full-Flavored Craft Beers." *Daily Oklahoman*, October 20, 2013. https://www.oklahoman.com/article/3895762/oklahomas-black-mesa-brewing-uses-science-to-brew-full-flavored-craft-beers?clearUserState=true.

"Start the Fight." *Custer County Clarion*, November 16, 1905, 7.

"State Craft Beer Brewers Group to Mark Oklahoma Repeal Day." *Daily Oklahoman*, April 7, 2016, 22.

"State Election on Beer Repeal Voted by House." *Daily Oklahoman*.

Sullivant, Otis. "State Beer Option Election Docketed for December 3." *Daily Oklahoman*, October 2, 1957, 1.

"Taxes Paid by Progress Brewery Aid State Schools." *Daily Oklahoman*, September 25, 1938, 100.

"Ten Cents a Bottle." *Daily Oklahoman*, September 3, 1904, 8.

Threadgill, Jacob. "Meet the Brewer: Black Mesa Brewing Company." *Oklahoma Gazette*, July 20, 2017. https://www.okgazette.com/oklahoma/meet-the-brewer-black-mesa-brewing-company/Content?oid=2980933.

Trougakos, Nick. "AB vs. Everybody." *Thirsty Beagle*, July 9, 2015. https://www.thirstybeagle.beer/2015/07/busy-beer-times-at-hand-in-oklahoma.html.

Bibliography

———. "Beer-Makers Look at Sales Growth Across State Lines." *Daily Oklahoman*, February 8, 2013, 17, 22.
———. "Bill Would Allow Liquor Stores to Sell Cold Beer." *Daily Oklahoman*, January 23, 2015, 26.
———. "Breweries to Benefit from State Proposal." *Daily Oklahoman*, January 28, 2015, 25, 28.
———. "Brewery in OKC Unveils Low-Point Canned Beers." *Daily Oklahoman*, October 29, 2014, 24.
———. "Choc Beer Tour Recap." *Daily Oklahoman*, March 29, 2010.
———. "City-Area Breweries Go to Web for Funds." *Daily Oklahoman*, January 12, 2013, 69, 74.
———. "COOP Shakes Up Staff, Moves Forward on Cans." *Daily Oklahoman*, September 24, 2010.
———. "Is Low-Point Beer Success on Tap for Area Breweries?" *Daily Oklahoman*, August 26, 2014, 23, 28.
———. "Krebs Brewery Helps Revive Polish Beer." *Daily Oklahoman*, April 18, 2012.
———. "Mustang Brewing to Buy OKCity Cooperative, Redbud Brand." *Daily Oklahoman*, November 13, 2012.
———. "Oklahoma Brewers Take Advantage of 3.2-Strength Beer Sales." *Daily Oklahoman*, August 26, 2014.
———. "Oklahoma City Brewing Cooperative Aims to Grow Beer Culture." *Daily Oklahoman*, August 3, 2012.
———. "Prairie Artisan Ales Continues to Make News." *Daily Oklahoman*. April 11, 2013.
———. "Redbud Brand to Continue After Departure of Brewmaster." *Daily Oklahoman*, August 31, 2012.
———. "The Scoop on Redbud Brewing Co." *Daily Oklahoman*, December 8, 2010.
———. "Storm Damage Leaves Three Oklahoma City Beer Brewers in the Dark." *Daily Oklahoman*, June 13, 2013.
———. "The Thirsty Beagle: A Conversation with JD Merryweather Previews Coop Ale in a Can." May 13, 2010. blog.newsok.com.
———. "This Just In: Cuvee One Is Pretty Awesome." *Daily Oklahoman*, February 12, 2011.
———. "What Does the Future Hold for Redbud Brewing Co.?" *Daily Oklahoman*, April 10, 2013.
Tucker, Kathy. "Last but Not Yeast: Cherry St.'s Brewer." *Tulsa World*, December 8, 1993. https://www.tulsaworld.com/archive/last-but-

Bibliography

not-yeast-cherry-sts-brewer/article_d5792804-0962-57f8-93f8-573dd638c70c.html.

"Tulsa Brew-Pub to Open." *Daily Oklahoman*, August 1, 1993, 46.

Tuttle, Ray. "Brewery Stock Sale Progressing." *Tulsa World*, March 9, 1993. https://www.tulsaworld.com/archive/brewery-stock-sale-progressing/article_21b515fd-6d50-5d22-9246-bb5f67327425.html.

"Wets Meet Today to Plan Campaign." *Daily Oklahoman*, October 3, 1957, 34.

Wofford, Jerry. "First Hop Jam Beer and Music Festival Set for Sunday." *Tulsa World*, May 15, 2014. https://tulsaworld.com/entertainment/music/first-hop-jam-beer-and-music-festival-set-for-sunday/article_5034270d-be48-56a3-a9a4-d6c82b9964fa.html.

———. "Hanson Talks About Mmmhops Beer Release." *Tulsa World*, November 22, 2013. https://tulsaworld.com/entertainment/music/hanson-talks-about-mmmhops-beer-elease/article_e109b648-53ba-11e3-ab6e-001a4bcf6878.html.

———. "Krebs Brewing Co. Acquires Tulsa-Based Prairie Artisan Ales." *Tulsa World*, June 30, 2016. https://tulsaworld.com/lifestyles/food-and-cooking/krebs-brewing-co-acquires-tulsa-based-prairie-artisanales/article_91db22c6-6fc5-5bc2-99e5-75ff8d3f363e.html.

Woodard, Nancy. "Where the Brewpubs Are." *Oklahoma Today* (March 1996): 56–66.

Wooley, John. "Brewfest Will Feature Barton, Sweeney Duo." *Tulsa World*, October 10, 1996. https://tulsaworld.com/archive/brewfest-will-feature-barton-sweeney-duo/article_9e77efb3-0b21-567e-8e98-b4b7443ff787.html.

Interviews

Much of the history presented here came from the author's podcast, which can be found at oklahomacraftbeer.com. All other personal interviews and recordings are in the possession of the author.

ABOUT THE AUTHOR

Brian Welzbacher has been a craft beer enthusiast and advocate since the early 2000s, while watching the St. Louis beer scene flourish. The Certified Beer Server enjoys being a stay-at-home dad to his daughter, Cora, and son, Rainn, while running his apparel and design company, Beer Is OK. He resides in Tulsa, Oklahoma, with his loving, beautiful and very understanding wife, Amy.

Visit us at
www.historypress.com

Printed in the USA
CPSIA information can be obtained
at www.ICGtesting.com
LVHW012041220224
772580LV00003B/94